TEACH
Them Diligently

a devotional guide for teachers

Arthur Nazigian

Published by:
The Christian Academy
3515 Edgmont Ave.
Brookhaven, Pa. 19015

Copyright 1974
by Arthur Nazigian
All rights reserved.

Cover Design by David A. McElwee

PRINTED IN THE UNITED STATES OF AMERICA

Dedicated . . .

to my dear wife, Ruth, and my three wonderful sons, Mark, Paul, and Jonathan. All of these are priceless possessions from the Lord. Bonded together in a Christian family, we teach each other and learn from each other every day as we grow and mature for God's glory.

CONTENTS

About the Author	vii
Preface	ix
Acknowledgments	xi
Introduction	1
Christian Education Begins	3
Biblical Profile of Education	5
Be Excited About Your School	7
The Classroom Body	9
Goal of Christian Education	12
First Things First	15
Undoing Miracles	17
Healed or Whole?	19
Discouragement . . . Deleted!	21
All Members are Vital	24
Only a Vapour	26
Lack of Money is Not the Problem	28
Divine Encounters	30
What's Needed, Lord?	32
Secret of Gaining Freedom	34
Thy Faith Hath Made Thee Whole	36
Everyone Witnesses Every Day	38
He was There Before	40
An Instrument	42
Satan's Circumstances	44
Words are Inexpensive	46
The Highest Calling	48
We Heard Him Ourselves	50
Downward Pull	52
God Did It	54
Completeness in Christ	56
Secular Education . . . Offense . . . or An Offense	60

Being a Powerful Servant	62
Jesus Employed in Your School	64
Problems Teach Lessons	66
Give No Offense	67
The Disciple of Christ	70
The Fields are Ready NOW!	73
True Love in School	75
Is a Child Worth It?	77
Keeping the Joy	80
One Pair of Eyes	82
Gaining Experience . . . Hope	84
Two Went up to Pray	86
How to Pray for Others	88
The Self Image	90
God's Will	92
Did You Ask?	95
Courage . . . Don't Ask!	97
The Student Becomes Like the Teacher	99
Teaching Truths Truthfully	101
God's Servant Must not Strive	103
Rise and Shine	105
One Story Only	107
What Has He Done for You!	109
Conclusion	111

ABOUT THE AUTHOR

"Art Nazigian is a man who loves the Saviour and who loves youth. I have seen these two qualities hundreds of times in the 15 years he has been associated with our camps at Schroon Lake, New York.

Art as a great athlete and with 22 years as an educator has a rich background from which he can draw experiences and insight into teaching youth the Word of God. Above all, he is one who still sticks to the good old paths and the ancient landmarks."

Dr. Jack Wyrtzen, Director
Word of Life International
Schroon Lake, New York

Mr. Arthur Nazigian received his Bachelor of Science in Education Degree from West Chester State Teachers College and his Master's Degree in Administration from the University of Pennsylvania. He has taken further graduate work beyond his Master's at the University of Delaware, Glassboro State and West Chester State Colleges.

His seven years as a teacher and six as a Principal in the public schools, include positions in the states of Pennsylvania and Delaware.

Prior to his coming to The Christian Academy in 1965 as Headmaster, he was directing a school in a northern suburb of Wilmington, Delaware.

Mr. Nazigian is currently the President of the Mid-Atlantic Christian School Association, which encompasses 150 Christian schools along the eastern seaboard. He has held this position since 1969.

Also, Mr. Nazigian is board member and an educational consultant for the National Christian School Education Association. He also serves on the faculty, each summer, of the National Institute of Christian School Administration conducted at Grace College, Winona Lake, Indiana.

Additional Christian work experience includes positions of Program Director, Word of Life Ranch; Word of Life Council member; Deacon; Chairman, Youth for Christ Board; Chairman, Youth Advisory Board and speaker on gospel teams.

Mr. Nazigian has played professional and semi-professional basketball for 10 years and was elected to the Delaware County, Pennsylvania, Basketball "Hall of Fame" in 1973.

Each year he is invited to speak at many Christian school functions, conferences, and sports banquets.

PREFACE

Each year I have the privilege of travelling to a number of Christian schools to speak to teachers, parents or to act as a resource person or to conduct a school evaluation. All of these functions bring me into close contact with many of the schools' personal areas of blessing and concern. It is simply amazing to see how vital the teacher is in the total process of education and how he is related to every phase of the school's program. Often we don't think of the teacher as having a crucial role in public relations, fund-raising, or generating school-wide love or enthusiasm, but he does. I have taken many portions of Scripture and drawn key practical applications that a teacher can understand and implement as he feels led.

I feel the position of the teacher must be highly regarded by those holding it and by those supporting it with their work and prayer. Since success can be attained by proper planning, God must always be in full control of this planning. Therefore, the Christian teacher must seek God's wisdom daily in all facets of his school life. At the heart of his daily work must be his sensitivity to the spiritual needs of his students. If a student has not opened his heart to Jesus Christ as Saviour, he must be prayed over and carefully led to make his decision. If the pupil needs to have his life totally yielded to the Lord or has any other key needs, the teacher has to be alert to help him. The Lord can provide this keen sensitivity that the teacher must have. The teacher has many other critical responsibilities and the Lord waits to provide the wisdom and direction needed. However, wisdom must be requested from God and His Word searched and studied.

The title, *Teach Them Diligently* is taken from Deuteronomy 6:7, "And thou shalt teach them diligently unto thy children...." This verse refers to taking God's Words, in the form of His Commandments, and fervently teaching them to our children in the morning, noon and night.

The verses and concepts you will read and meditate upon in this book represent almost two years of work locating these teaching principles and sharing them with my staff during morning devotions. I have only uncovered a very small number of these valuable directives from His Word. Many more "scriptural nuggets" are waiting to be discovered and used to make teaching more exciting and productive.

I would be most happy to hear from those who find the book helpful in their own lives and schools.

Art Nazigian, Headmaster
The Christian Academy
Brookhaven, Pa. 19015

ACKNOWLEDGMENTS

A work of this nature is usually accomplished because of the cooperative efforts of a number of individuals. This book is no exception. I am especially grateful to the following friends for all their labor in Christian love for God's glory:

>Jean and Bill Wooster
>Lois and Don Weaver
>Randy Carroll
>John Cerrato
>Richard Cavallini

INTRODUCTION

If you serve God as a Christian school teacher, this book is for you. It is true to the Word of God, practical, and relevant to the daily experiences of teaching. This is not a book which you will read only once, but is one which you will read periodically. It will become a valued book in your professional library, well marked.

Each of us wants to be a complete Christian teacher, not just a Christian who is also a teacher. To be complete, we need to be properly integrated teachers who perceive the relationships between the Bible and all of our educational work. This perception is not automatic because we are Christians, but it is developed as we study books which cause us to think through our teaching from the Bible's viewpoint. We need this, for our own education was primarily from the viewpoint of man's reason, not from the viewpoint of God's revelation. Teachers must be re-educated to be complete Christian teachers.

Art Nazigian is a leader in Christian school education, serving in positions of regional and national leadership in addition to the administration of his own school. He is a sensitive Christian, and this comes through in his writing. *Teach Them Diligently* is a record of spiritual lessons which God has taught him over a period of years. These truths are now being shared with all of us in God's School System for our example.

We want to honor the Lord Jesus Christ in our Christian schools. You and I will do this more effectively by practicing these spiritual instructions and exhortations.

Roy W. Lowrie, Jr.
Newtown Square, Pennsylvania
Executive Director,
National Christian School Educational Association

1

CHRISTIAN EDUCATION BEGINS

And the Lord God took the man, and put him into the Garden of Eden to dress it and to keep it.

And the Lord God commanded the man, saying, Of every tree of the garden thou mayest freely eat:

But of the tree of the knowledge of good and evil, thou shalt not eat of it: for in the day that thou eatest thereof thou shalt surely die. *Genesis 2:15-17*

What a beautiful picture of the first educational scene! God has just created the Garden of Eden with all its beauty and splendor and now He instructs man, His highest creation. He teaches man about the various aspects of the Garden; how to dress it, keep it, what to eat, and then His final instructions about the tree of the knowledge of good and evil. God was the very first teacher, and man the pupil. The questions raised at this point could well be, "Why did God begin with man?" "What is man anyway?"

Psalm 8:5-9 answers, "What is man?"

The rest of God's Word reveals to us the deep love of God to man. Love for the pupil has to be in the heart of the teacher and at the heart of his daily work, if he is to be an effective teacher.

In Genesis 2:19, 20, amazingly God brings the beasts of the field and the fowls of the air to Adam to see what he would name them. Adam named the animals. God allows man to be creative. He wants man to be original. God's desire is that we have great freedom to glorify Him; however, all of our liberty must be within the confines and limits of His Word.

God is still at His teaching post. In the Old Testament He is God, the Father, teaching us by actual example; in the New Testament He is God, the Son, teaching by precept; today He is God, the Holy Spirit, teaching us by holy inspiration through His Word.

The Christian teacher has the perfect example of the Master Teacher. As we recognize the Lordship of Jesus Christ in our lives and are fully yielded to Him, He structures our lives to produce much fruit in our school work.

Since God knows each pupil in your class better than you do, He is willing to impart that knowledge to you. You must pray for the insights and wisdom needed each day. Have a prayer conference today and every day, with the very first Teacher. . . .

2

BIBLICAL PROFILE OF EDUCATION

And thou shalt love the Lord thy God with all thine heart, and with all thy soul, and with all thy might.

And these words, which I command thee this day, shall be in thine heart:

And thou shalt teach them diligently unto thy children, and shalt talk of them when thou sittest in thine house, and when thou walkest by the way, and when thou liest down, and when thou risest up.

And thou shalt bind them for a sign upon thine hand, and they shall be as frontlets between thine eyes.

And thou shalt write them upon the posts of thy house, and on thy gates. *Deuteronomy 6:5-9*

As one views the entire Bible, he does not see schools, as we know them today, mentioned anywhere. There are some scattered verses about teachers in the temples, teaching those dedicated to the priesthood.

However, there are many portions of Scripture that give a pattern for the education of the family. Deuteronomy 6:5-9 succinctly does this. The heart of the training process for children is that God's commandments must be on continuous review before the children. In the morning while arising; sitting in the house; walking to and fro; all during the day; in the evening hours; while lying down, God's commandments are to be on parade. This is done by speaking of His love, by showing His graces, by reading His Word, and by all other ways living His commandments before the children.

Some other scriptural references to this same concept are:

But His delight is in the law of the Lord; and in His law doth he meditate day and night (Ps. 1:2).

Thy word have I hid in mind heart that I might not sin against Thee (Ps. 119:11).

In all thy ways acknowledge Him and He shall direct thy paths (Prov. 3:6).

Whether therefore ye eat or drink, or whatsoever ye do, do all to the glory of God (I Cor. 10:31).

Let this mind be in you, which was also in Christ Jesus (Phil. 2:5).

Due to the highly technical aspects of education, parents have to turn their children over to someone else with a professional background of learning, to take their place as teachers. In fact, it was the secular system of schools that coined the truth "in loco parentis" (in place of the parent).

You as the teacher replace the parent during the day. God's profile of education, however, is not to be "shelved" for thirty daylight hours a week but it is to be continuous. God wants you to take the reins of the children's learning program and keep His commandments on daily review....

3

BE EXCITED ABOUT YOUR SCHOOL

Servants, obey in all things your masters according to the flesh; not with eyeservice, as menpleasers; but in singleness of heart, fearing God:

And whatsoever ye do, do it heartily, as to the Lord, and not unto men;

Knowing that of the Lord ye shall receive the reward of the inheritance: for ye serve the Lord Christ.
Colossians 3:22-24

Emerson tells us: "Every great and commanding movement in the annals of the world is the triumph of enthusiasm. Nothing great was ever accomplished without it."

Paul says, "Whatsoever ye do, do it heartily as to the Lord."

Emerson expounds the success of enthusiasm, while Paul reveals the secret of it ... *as to the Lord.*

Enthusiasm can be contagious! It can spread to you and stop or it can spread through you to others. Your attitude is the key. How do you view your teaching responsibilities before the Lord? Are you working for the Board ... for the Principal ... or for the Lord? We are to obey those in authority, of course, for the Scriptures make this clear. However, we need to realize without any reservation that we are laboring for the Lord Himself. We tell those about us that we are in Christian Service, but in reality we sometimes deny this in our daily work. Each day is a low enthusiasm, high complaint time with little trials tripping us constantly. We are quick to discern faults and only too willing to identify their owners.

The challenge is not just to spiritualize in talk only, but to open our "spiritual eyes" to see God's hand at work in our school. He is doing wonderful things for each of our schools daily. Do we see Him working? Pray for enthusiasm! Engulf your whole personality with it . . . it can be done!

Your life can be a self-generating enthusiasm unit. You can stir up excitement in others with your example. Renew your mind by conditioning your thinking to face daily problems with a fresh enthusiasm. Remember in all things . . . give thanks. He reigns!

Walk a little faster today with your head higher. Learn to smile often and laugh a lot! You say it's the Lord's battle or the Lord's work and then turn around and act as though it were yours! Think of some ways you can encourage and excite others in your school. Turn others on by turning yourself on! You have a very exciting school, so be thankful and let your praise have power!

4

THE CLASSROOM BODY

Now there are diversities of gifts, but the same Spirit.

And there are differences of administrations, but the same Lord.

And there are diversities of operations, but it is the same God which worketh all in all.

But the manifestation of the Spirit is given to every man to profit withal. *I Corinthians 12:4-7*

For as the body is one, and hath many members, and all the members of that one body, being many, are one body: so also is Christ.

For by one Spirit are we all baptized into one body, whether we be Jews or Gentiles, whether we be bond or free; and have been all made to drink into one Spirit.

For the body is not one member, but many.
I Corinthians 12:12-14

One of the vital truths of I Corinthians 12 is that through our faith in Jesus Christ, we become part of His Body. When God puts together a group of believers, then they are to function as one effective unit, even though there will be notable differences. A classroom in a Christian School would be no different. Within that room are all the parts of the body to function in unison for the Lord. To expect a classroom of students to perform as an eye alone, or as an arm alone, is not logical before the Lord. As teachers, we are to evaluate our students through prayer, asking God for wisdom in planning and programming.

We should work to locate the strengths and

weaknesses in each child. To motivate the child to use his strengths to help the weakness of others becomes the ministry within the ministry. We know that in an average classroom, all of the students are not going to be "A" students. In fact, they are not all going to enter college nor are they all going to become craftsmen. All are not leaders and all are not followers. Realizing these differences, our task is to get the class to function as a spiritual body in the midst of an educational endeavor.

Academically, we are to challenge each student to do his best. To work diligently, to complete assignments, to work neatly and carefully; these are certainly within the grasp of each student. However, to expect them all to be honor-roll students is not within their reach.

Spiritually, we should use those with leadership potential as leaders, while those who are good followers as followers.

There are those that love to serve and help others. Some are teachers, some are gifted in other ways, and so it goes among the believers. God will show us how these students dovetail together to aid and encourage one another. It becomes very exciting to work to put this body together and then to see it function for Christ day after day. Also, remember all of the parts of the body are not as pleasing to the eye as other parts, but all are very necessary!

That there should be no schism in the body; but that the members should have the same care one for another.

And whether one member suffer, all the members suffer with it; or one member be honoured, all the members rejoice with it.

Now ye are the body of Christ, and members in particular.
I Corinthians 12:25-27

Think of the great potential your class represents . . . and YOU are in charge!

5

GOAL OF CHRISTIAN EDUCATION

Where there is no vision, the people perish: but he that keepeth the law, happy is he. *Proverbs 29:18*

According to the grace of God which is given unto me, as a wise masterbuilder, I have laid the foundation, and another buildeth thereon. But let every man take heed how he buildeth thereupon.

For other foundation can no may lay than that is laid, which is Jesus Christ. *I Corinthians 3:10, 11*

For who hath known the mind of the Lord, that he may instruct him? But we have the mind of Christ.

I Corinthians 2:16

In order for any work of Christ to be truly effective, a definite goal has to be established. What is the goal of daily Christian education? Exactly what type of student is the school trying to produce?

In Philippians 2:5, we read, "Let this mind be in you, which was also in Christ Jesus." This verse clearly and succinctly indicates the ultimate goal of the Christian School in regard to its final product. *The chief end of the school is to produce a boy or girl who has the mind of Christ.*

First, in order to have the mind of Jesus Christ, he must, of course, be *in* Christ. Therefore, the salvation of each student is imperative. The school is basically teaching for the initial decision, if one has never been made. After one receives Jesus Christ into his life as his own personal Saviour, he is then able with the proper teaching, based on the Word of God, to develop the mind of Christ.

What comprises the mind of Christ? What areas

of life does Christ consider vital? In Luke 2:52, it states, "Jesus increased in wisdom and stature, and in favor with God and man."

Four areas are noted to which Jesus Christ gave attention; mental, physical, spiritual, and social. Christ was illustrating that each of these four areas is important to the effective existence of man.

In the mental phase, to have the mind of Christ means to be attuned to the thinking of the Creator. Who formed the stars for the astronomy class or the planets for outer space study? Who fashioned the mountains and animals for the studies in geology and biology? Who gave the logical sequence to numbers to create mathematics? Who allowed the men and women to enter this world to set in motion the wheels of history? God Almighty is responsible for these phenomena! To have the mind of Christ, the Creator, entails a deeper, richer understanding of everything around us. It means developing and maintaining a desire for academic knowledge.

In the physical realm, to have the mind of Christ means that one would understand and respect his body as the temple of the Holy Spirit (I Cor. 3:16). This means that the Temple must be carefully and prayerfully treated through proper rest, food, exercise, and other good health habits. The abstinence from tobacco, alcohol, drugs, and so forth, is essential to do God's work effectively and for a longer duration. Sports and recreation have an important and rightful place in the curriculum.

Socially, the mind of Christ reasons that we are

all God's creations. Therefore, one human is not above another. We are all sinners who can be saved by grace. We must love one another regardless of race, color, or creed. Out of a heart of love and compassion for one another, we help and comfort others while guiding and protecting them; eventually winning them to Jesus Christ.

Lastly, in the spiritual area, to have the mind of Christ is to have the desire Jesus did in John 8:29b, when He stated, "... I do always those things that please Him." Christ's desire was to do the will of His Father. This is the chief spiritual goal of the school: to produce the boy or girl who wants to please his heavenly Father by being directly in the center of His will ... a boy or girl who is daily walking by faith in the Holy Spirit. As the Lord guides this young person, whether for daily living or for a vocation, he will be open and receptive to his Father's will.

The mind of Christ is not automatically given to His born-again children. The mind of Christ must be taught and developed systematically by the Word, through prayer, through constant example.

You as the classroom teacher must realize how vital your role is in teaching. You are the visual object lesson for the pupil each day. Therefore, your life has to be that consistent example the child needs. The Student will learn and absorb the mind of Christ ... as You reflect it daily.

6

FIRST THINGS FIRST

Therefore if thou bring thy gift to the altar, and there rememberest that thy brother hath ought against thee;

Leave there thy gift before the altar, and go thy way; first be reconciled to thy brother, and then come and offer thy gift. *Matthew 5:23, 24*

Christians by the millions are at the altar of sacrifice each day. They love the Lord and are willing to give up money, time, physical effort, and anything else for the "Cause of Christ." However, God asks why you are here if you have ought against your brother. Can you think of a student, parent, fellow-teacher, board member, relative, or a friend that stirs your negative emotions when you think of him? Is there a "twinge" of bitterness or resentment when you think of one or more of these? If there is, then God says you need to leave the altar, make things right and then come back to worship and serve.

The Word does not state that if you are wrong you should seek out your brother. It simply says you must make things right. It will take courage to go to the person, tell him your attitudes were wrong, that you are sorry, and ask for forgiveness. What a great flow of joy and blessing will follow! It will be like a dam of ill feelings, thoughts, and negative actions exploding and opening the way for the Holy Spirit and the love of God to fill you, and cause you to be of greater service to Him.

On the love of God and the love of others hang

all the laws and prophets. When we let our emotions be governed by the flesh, or argue, destructively criticize, or deal harshly with others, we create obstructions in our lives that quickly dam up God's love. This love is to flow through us daily to reach others with the message of salvation or the message of comfort and help.

To keep our spiritual channels open, we must follow I John 1:9:

If we confess our sins, he is faithful and just to forgive us our sins, and to cleanse us from all unrighteousness.

We must be in a continual state of being sensitive to sin and quickly confessing it if we fall. However, we can't say, "Well, we'll start now to follow this pattern." We must go back, and as we think of others we have offended, we must seek their forgiveness and then we will start to see and feel the wonderful love of God move out from us to our classes and from our classes to the rest of the world.

Release a spiritual prisoner from jail today . . . YOU! If you stay in the bondage of past unloving actions or attitudes without making amends, you become ineffective in communicating God's truths daily. You can prepare your lessons and give out the Word clearly, but it will not make the necessary impact you want it to upon the students. Christians, especially teachers, yearn to know and share warmly God's love. If this is going to happen, then you must be reconciled to your brother as God has told you to be.

Go back to others . . . to come up to God's best for you.

7

UNDOING MIRACLES

Then again called they the man that was blind, and said unto him, Give God the praise: we know that this man is a sinner.

He answered and said, Whether he be a sinner or no, I know not: one thing I know, that, whereas I was blind, now I see.

Then said they to him again, What did he to thee? How opened he thine eyes?

He answered them, I have told you already, and ye did not hear: wherefore would ye hear it again? Will ye also be his disciples?

Then they reviled him, and said, Thou are his disciple; but we are Moses' disciples. *John 9:24-28*

Here was a clear case of a complete miracle, yet the Pharisees were so bent on undoing the miracle that they badgered the formerly blind man to give a full account of the healing. They were trying to show that it was not a miracle. However, the healed man could do nothing but repeat the same story.

God is working miracles today. As one views the operation of our schools, he sees how teachers are being sent; how parents are able to meet tuition payments; how finances are being obtained to balance budgets; and how land and buildings are continually acquired. Each story has miraculous overtones, and yet there are skeptics, in spite of all they see.

These doubters ask, "How did the money come in to pay for the building?" You go over the story again of how the Lord provided. They insist on minute details believing that the miracle can easily be explained away.

Just as the healed man did, we need to stick to the miracle story, to praise and thank God, and to continue to serve Him. Also, we need to develop a "spirit of expectancy" for further miracles. God does not stop with one or two. He will continue to provide just so long as the needs are there and faith is being exercised.

The children of Israel experienced miracle after miracle. It was their unbelief, the complaining, and groaning that possibly short-circuited many more miracles that God would have performed. Why not rejoice right now in a special way, thank the Lord for what He has done, and pray earnestly for a new miracle to grace the school?

God is more concerned about your needs than you could ever be . . . and it will take a miracle to meet some of those needs. You can undo a miracle in two ways. One is simply to explain it away. The other is not to pray for it or not to expect it. In either case, you miss one of the finest blessings that the Lord can provide. Instead of sitting in the grandstands watching God's hand working miracles, why not enter into the arena and be a part of the miracle? With prayers, with faith, and with a sense of keen anticipation, you can help to bring it about.

"Expect a miracle" is a sign that faces those who sit across from my desk at school. The back of the sign reads, "Jesus Only" . . . as the answer to how the miracle can be accomplished.

As a dear child of God, you are as eligible as anyone to ask for and to receive a miracle for your school. Why not pray for something big to happen to your school today!

8

HEALED OR WHOLE?

And as he entered into a certain village, there met him ten men that were lepers, which stood afar off:

And they lifted up their voices, and said, Jesus, Master, have mercy on us.

And when he saw them, he said unto them, Go shew yourselves unto the priests. And it came to pass, that, as they went, they were cleansed.

And one of them, when he saw that he was healed, turned back, and with a loud voice glorified God,

And fell down on his face at his feet, giving him thanks: and he was a Samaritan.

And Jesus answering said, Were there not ten cleansed? but where are the nine?

There are not found that returned to give glory to God, save this stranger.

And he said unto him, Arise, go thy way: thy faith hath made thee whole. *Luke 17:12-19*

Ten lepers appeal to Jesus and He heals them all, but only one leaves healed *and whole.* Only one leper thanked the Lord and expressed a saving faith in the Saviour. Here was one who was made whole in body and spirit.

It is very easy day after day in dealing with our school children to be more concerned about their healing rather than their wholeness. We see student problems in reading, math, or science; a boy or girl who is constantly giving us "discipline headaches"; a parent always on the telephone about one issue after another. All of these need healing . . . and do they need something more? They say that a troublesome person is generally . . . *a person in trouble!*

We, as Christian teachers, need to be primarily interested in one's soul first. We need to be soul winners daily! We must strive to lead that boy or girl or parent to Jesus Christ, and to be sure his relationship to Him is proper. We need to be sure the person is *whole* first. Often the *healing* of the problems will result later. Use each problem as an opening to get to heart issues. Sometimes even academic problems can be solved with the spiritual area being taken care of first.

One day a small ten-year old boy who had already lived in several orphanage homes, and had been transferred because of his troublesome ways, walked across the playground of a school. When he reached the high fence, he climbed up and reached over and placed a note in a tree limb that was hanging over the yard. A teacher, watching him, quickly went and climbed the fence to get the note. When the note was opened, it read, "Whoever finds this note, I love you!"

The little lad knew trouble and the many forms of discipline that accompanied it; however, he had never experienced the most vital quality of discipline . . . love. Everyone was trying to heal the boy of his troublesome ways, but no one was concerned about his *wholeness.*

Help someone to shape up today to be a whole person . . . in Jesus Christ!

. . . ye are complete in him (Col. 2:10).

9

DISCOURAGEMENT . . . DELETED!

And be not drunk with wine, wherein is excess; but be filled with the Spirit;

Speaking to yourselves in psalms and hymns and spiritual songs, singing and *making melody in your heart to the Lord;*

Giving thanks always for all things unto God and the Father in the name of our Lord Jesus Christ.   *Ephesians 5:18-20*

There is an old story telling about a senior devil getting ready to retire. He was putting all his tools up for sale, hoping some young aspirant would take over his work where he finished! One day a junior devil was looking over the various tools noting the prices. "Jealousy," "resentment," "gossip" all were quite expensive. Suddenly, junior spotted an old, very worn tool with the highest price tag of all. "What is this that is worth so much?" he asked the old timer.

With a proud smile senior said, "This is the tool I used most. I have ruined, defeated, or at least slowed down more Christians and their ministries with this than with all my other vices put together. That my boy . . . is *discouragement!*"

Discouragement says that Ephesians 5:18-20 is not true! We should not be making melody in our hearts and thanking God always for all things.

You say, "I'm not sure if God knows what happened to ruin my day . . . my plan . . . my program. If He were aware, then why did it happen? What's the use!"

Another potentially powerful human force for Christ comes to a grinding halt!

Determine in your heart you will not become discouraged under any circumstances. Even if you experience several serious setbacks successively, purpose that you will praise the power of the peerless person of Christ . . . Master of all . . . men and situations.

One afternoon as I was driving home from school after an unusually taxing day of sticky problems, I was close to the point of discouragement. However, I remembered that when I first entered Christian School work, I promised myself, before the Lord, that I would under no circumstances become discouraged. So, instead of continuing to look to myself, I turned to Him. My "hang-up" was this, "Lord, if Christian Education is ordained of you with so many Scriptures to substantiate it, why are Christian Schools besieged with so many problems?"

I waited upon the Lord for the answer to this puzzling question. The answer came clearly in the form of a question. The Lord asked, "Where on the battle field is the fighting the hottest?" Obviously, the war rages fiercely at the most strategic positions, those critical strongholds where the advantage would be the greatest for those who occupy them.

Next to gaining the *heart*, gaining the *minds* of boys and girls is the greatest pursuit of life. Satan battles with every ounce of strength to keep the heart and mind of individuals, especially children. If he succeeds, he conquers this life. However, if one chooses Christ, then a new, vibrant, abundant, and eternal life is secured.

The Christian School strives daily to gain the hearts and minds of children for the glory of God ... in reaching the souls of men.

Are you discouraged? You are in the greatest work of all for the Lord ... keep up your joy ... the best is yet to come!

10

ALL MEMBERS ARE VITAL

For as the body is one, and hath many members, and all the members of that one body, being many, are one body: so also is Christ.

For the body is not one member but many.

If the foot shall say, Because I am not the hand, I am not of the body; is it therefore not of the body?

And if the ear shall say, Because I am not the eye, I am not of the body; is it therefore not of the body?

If the whole body were an eye, where were the hearing? If the whole were the hearing, where were the smelling?

But now hath God set the members every one of them in the body, as it hath pleased him. *I Corinthians 12:12, 14-18*

From these portions of Scripture we see that God fits the body together and that all parts are important to the total function of the body. The eye is vital to see with, but if the entire body were an eye, how could it carry out any other function? On the other hand, if the body were an ear or a leg only, how could it see?

If a beautiful wristwatch were held up, and the question asked, "Which part of the watch is the most important?" the answer would be clear. Every part is important. Everyone sees the hands and the sparkling case; however, if one little spring in the back does not work, the entire watch stops.

In a Christian School, the board chairman, the principal, and other key leaders are the ones most often on view. However, everyone is necessary to the efficient operation, even those behind the scenes. If a bus driver, a secretary, or a custodian fails, the whole organization could be seriously hindered or possibly halted. Each team member must realize his own importance before the Lord and act accordingly. He, in turn, must be treated with the same love and respect as those in higher positions.

This is not to say that everyone's responsibilities are the same. The principal encounters much more pressure than would a bus driver or custodian; however, each must do his respective job properly if God is to be honored and the work is to progress. The team spirit idea is not just a "pep rally principle" but has real substance to it.

The Christian School is a definite team. God is the Owner. The Board is the manager. The Principal is the captain.

Go forth today with a new zeal and a new desire to be the best in your respective position . . . because the Owner is always with you.

11

ONLY A VAPOUR

Whereas ye know not what shall be on the morrow. For what is your life? It is even a vapour, that appeareth for a little time, and then vanisheth away. *James 4:14*

And as it is appointed unto men once to die, but after this the judgment: *Hebrews 9:27*

So teach us to number our days, that we may apply our hearts unto wisdom. *Psalm 90:12*

It was a warm sunny afternoon when I pulled up to the small suburban church. The funeral service was already in session! The duet was singing "It is Well With My Soul" and the group of friends and loved ones sat in a semicomatose state. Then the very familiar, "Just as I am," concluded the singing.

It was very difficult to realize that "Rick" was gone at nineteen years of age, knowing that it was a policeman's bullet that had put the period to his life. My own emotions were deeply disturbed, especially because "Rick" had been a student in our Christian School from age ten to fourteen. He was basically a nice, lovable boy, but was always in some difficulty with the teachers. He had a good mind, but was very undisciplined in his life. His home was a continuous battleground, between a mother who loved the Lord and was trying hard to guide the family with the Bible, and a father who didn't care about God. Every child in the family was torn with divided allegiance among the father, mother, and the school.

On one occasion when Rick was sent to me for

discipline, I had the opportunity to lead him to Jesus Christ. I felt his decision was sincere; however, he just didn't grow. The deep turmoil at home was too distracting to his emotional state. He just couldn't turn his life over to the Lord. Later he dropped out of Christian School and finished his last years in the local secular high school.

Rick is in heaven today not because of his own life, but due to the life and death of Jesus Christ. My own heartache is to think about the potential this boy's life represented to the cause of Christ. If we, as a staff, knew he was going to come to this end, would we have done more for him? Is it possible that we would have gone another mile or two with him? Eternity will reveal these answers. However, we need to be awake now to our students.

You have been challenged to think you may have a future D. L. Moody or a C. H. Spurgeon in your class, but you need, also, to be aware that a pool of violent blood may await some of your students. You need to pray more earnestly for wisdom; and then, with love, to work diligently with each child, because life is only a vapour which appears and then vanishes. What you must do, you must do quickly!

12

LACK OF MONEY IS NOT THE PROBLEM

For every beast of the forest is mine, and the cattle upon a thousand hills. *Psalm 50:10*

The silver is mine, and the gold is mine, saith the Lord of hosts. *Haggai 2:8*

If Christian school leaders and staff were asked, "What is the number one problem of the Christian School?" the immediate answer would undoubtedly be, "Money!"

The lack of money certainly has many Christian schools reeling and wondering what is going to happen next. It has brought more schools to their knees than any five other problems combined. Therefore, money is crucial, but it is not number one! Rarely does the Bible list the lack of money as a serious problem. One of the few accounts is written below with a swift solution. In reference to money for paying taxes, Jesus speaks in Matthew 17:27 and says:

Notwithstanding, lest we should offend them, go thou to the sea, and cast an hook, and take up the fish that first cometh up; and when thou hast opened his mouth, thou shalt find a piece of money: take that, and give unto them for me and thee.

Our Christian schools lack money because of our number one problem . . . *lack of prayer!* Prayer is the heart and the power core of the school. We have not because we ask not. Since we all have a nucleus of prayer warriors, our schools do progress and weather the storm.

"Much prayer . . . much power" is the title of a

book. This title alone speaks volumes of truth which we need. If only we could get each family member of the school to pray earnestly daily, what a difference we would see! God would touch hearts to give; other hearts would be touched to work; still others would receive wisdom and understanding to save or make money for the school; and so it goes on, with God giving.

Prayer *before* planning is always the proper order. So often we get an idea, and plan how it can be implemented; then we start praying that God will bless the project. Later we may start listing reasons why the project was not too successful.

Careful prayer and consideration need to be given to each idea to raise funds. When the conviction that it is God's will to go ahead becomes apparent, then the plans can be laid. Hard work needs to be employed by all. Every facet of the project must be engulfed in prayer. Brainstorm ways to get more people to *pray*.

God has millions and millions of dollars. He has no shortage of funds. He has invested these funds in Christians. Christians need to pray fervently that God will release hearts to give according to His will.

The lack of money is often due to the lack of prayer. The prayers of many are needed.

As a teacher, you should pray for the funds to come in to your school. Encourage your children to do the same. You cannot delegate, in your mind, the task of money raising to your school board or to your principal. You must do your share by earnestly asking God to release the money needed to keep the school strong and progressing for the Lord.

13

DIVINE ENCOUNTERS

And let us consider one another to provoke unto love and to good works.
Hebrews 10:24

Each person is programmed to do his own thing! Almost like a computer individuals go about their work daily with little or no regard for incidents, and even accidents, which occur around them. Interruptions are viewed with an irritable, suspicious eye. On one hand the thought is, "What is this all about?" On the other hand, "How can I quickly get through this situation?"

Has one ever considered the fact that all time is God's time and that He is ultimately in charge of all schedules? If He chooses to interrupt one's work, one needs to be conscious that there may be a greater work of ministry to do at the moment. As the verse tells us, we need to consider one another to provoke (to motivate) someone unto love and to good works.

One night, a man of the Pharisees named Nicodemus, a ruler of the Jews, came to Jesus. It can be said with almost certainty that he did not have an appointment! Yet Jesus took time to deal with him and point this leader to several eternal truths.

In another situation, Jesus was walking and ministering to the masses when suddenly a rich young ruler came running to Him. Interrupting the Lord, he wanted to know the answer to a vital question. Jesus took time to deal with this individual and through love challenged him to good works.

One day while Jesus was in the temple, a lawyer stood up and asked a question unrelated to the discussion at hand. Jesus met the interruption with understanding and vital truth.

Everyone needs to plan his work . . . then work his plan. However, others have to be considered and if interruptions occur, they must be quickly evaluated since Satan is ever trying to slow down God's work.

When there is a clear-cut opportunity to minister to someone physically, academically, or spiritually, you must be ready to accept God's challenge. Allow His love to flow through you . . . provoking others to love and to good works.

Preach the word; be instant in season, *out of season;* reprove, rebuke, exhort with all longsuffering and doctrine (II Tim. 4:2).

14

WHAT'S NEEDED, LORD?

Take heed to yourselves: If thy brother trespass against thee, rebuke him; and if he repent, forgive him.

And if he trespass against thee seven times in a day, and seven times in a day turn again to thee, saying, I repent; thou shalt forgive him.

And the apostles said unto the Lord, Increase our faith.
Luke 17:3-5

Here was a situation where the Lord challenged His own disciples to a greater step of service. He explained that as the children of God, they must have enough compassion to forgive over and over again without number as long as there was a spirit of repentance. The disciples were quick to see their deficiency and instead of rationalizing or excusing themselves with some philosophical explanation, they quickly got to the point of the problem. That their faith was not strong enough to have this kind of love was evident, so they cried ... "Lord, increase our faith."

God's Word is a many-splendored gift! Among other things, it is a mirror of one's soul. Often we can see the weaknesses in our lives that need attention. As we labor in our schools each day, we need to be open to the Holy Spirit's conviction. He will reveal what we must do so that we may become what He wants us to be. Are we willing to cry aloud unto the Lord to make the corrections within ourselves as did the disciples?

One evening as I was concluding my message at

a nearby mission, I had a real surprise. I had reached the invitation and had just finished explaining, "accepting Jesus Christ." One man jumped up and bellowed, "I'll receive Him—I'll receive Him—I want Him for my Saviour!" I was a little stumped to see such a quick, immediate response. The man saw his need and reached out to God without wasting a second.

God will continue to reveal new truth as we accept it. If we hear His voice . . . possibly through a verse of Scripture, and choose to sidetrack the issue, He will withhold new truth. He will go into a drill session for us and try to teach us the same truth another way. Over and over the truth will come, in one way or another, until we do receive it. It is a sad thing to see an older Christian who is still in the primary grades in the spiritual school of life.

Call out the answer as you see it come from the Lord. Ask and ye shall receive!

15

SECRET OF GAINING FREEDOM

And when they had laid many stripes upon them, they cast them into prison, charging the jailor to keep them safely:

Who, having received such a charge, thrust them into the inner prison, and made their feet fast in the stocks.

And at midnight Paul and Silas prayed, and sang praises unto God: and the prisoners heard them.

And suddenly there was a great earthquake, so that the foundations of the prison were shaken: and immediately all the doors were opened, and every one's bands were loosed.
Acts 16:23-26

The prospects for freedom were bleak! Paul and Silas were beaten and imprisoned with the intention of retaining them. However, Paul had the keys to freedom. He had *prayer* and *praise*. As soon as they prayed and sang praises to God, their spirits were released; released from despair, disappointment, and dismay! They had a joy in the midst of pain and gloom, knowing they were under God's love, serving Him, counting it a privilege to suffer for Him.

Physical release also came quickly! In fact, God honored Paul and Silas with a mighty fanfare testimony as He sent an earthquake to do the job that could have been done with a lesser force. However, there was another reason for the earthquake! It opened all the other doors of the prison as well as awakening the keeper. God further expanded the spiritual opportunities of Paul and Silas by giving them the jail keeper and his house for eternity.

When a school situation has a binding effect

upon us, we need to quickly use the keys of prayer and praise for release! The situation may be in relation to a classroom problem, a school rule or program, or a board policy. Possibly, we may be tied in knots because of an individual student, a fellow teacher, or someone in the administration. Whatever is the case, we have no freedom because this thing is continually filling our mind with a chain of thoughts.

The keys to freedom are prayer and praise! We must pray, confessing our faults; thanking God for this situation; asking for wisdom; allowing understanding to replace resentment. Praise, according to His righteousness, then follows naturally; praising God for His love, His faithfulness, His holiness, His perfection, His righteous judgments, His vengeance, His guidance, His power, *His will.*

Your release and joy are the natural results if you use these keys as did the Apostle Paul in his most trying circumstances. Another amazing result takes place. Not only you, but the object of your attention is also released. That person or situation can then move freely to be corrected, changed, or continued, in accordance with God's perfect will . . . which is all to be desired anyway. . . .

16

THY FAITH HATH MADE THEE WHOLE

And Jesus said, Somebody hath touched me: for I perceive that virtue is gone out of me.

And when the woman saw that she was not hid, she came trembling, and falling down before him, she declared unto him before all the people for what cause she had touched him, and how she was healed immediately.

And he said unto her, Daughter, be of good comfort: thy faith hath made thee whole; go in peace.   *Luke 8:46-48*

In this particular case, a physically sick woman was made whole because of her faith in the living Saviour. Is it possible that wholeness can come to other areas of our life, or of our school's life through the exercise of faith?

I feel our Lord is certainly the Master of all! The principle of faith is overwhelming in potential power. The Book of Hebrews begins with a good definition of faith and then proceeds to give illustration after illustration of different people in different circumstances exercising this faith with startling results. Faith has unlimited power when it is released.

If the lack of funds is a problem, first there must be prayer and then a large faith step of some type. If personnel, program, or parents are in some way deficient, then a faith project, originated in prayer and given support by the necessary school officials, is the key to bringing wholeness of results to the situation.

It is impossible, of course, for school persons

or others to affirm to individuals exactly how faith projects will work for each school. Circumstances differ from school to school and from situation to situation. We are certain to find inspiration, however, in similar circumstances of the past, of prayer's effectiveness for our guidance.

Each of our schools desires to please God. We want every facet of our ministry to be blessed and directed of the Lord. Then, without question, Hebrews 11:6 must be fully embraced: "But without faith, it is impossible to please him: for He that cometh to God must believe that He is, and that He is a rewarder of them that diligently seek Him.

How pleasing is your school to the Lord?
How much faith are you exercising?
What is your latest faith project?
Have you need of healing? . . . Thy faith will make you whole!

17

EVERYONE WITNESSES EVERY DAY

Ye are my witnesses, saith the Lord, and my servant whom I have chosen: that ye may know and believe me, and understand that I am he: before me there was no God formed, neither shall there be after me.

I, even I, am the Lord; and beside me there is no Saviour.

Isaiah 43:10, 11

So often, in our Christian walk, we are challenged to "witness" for Jesus Christ, to lead a soul to eternal life. We start to feel as though witnessing can be turned on or off, depending on our spiritual temperature and on our own desire. We don't realize that everything in existence, every day, gives witness to God Almighty, even to the individual who has turned his back on the Lord. If we could look deep into a person's life who has not accepted Jesus Christ, we would see that the person's entire life is a testimony. His life would be devoid of hope and joy. We would see what happens to a life that rejects God's Word.

Our lives today, as born-again Christians, speak loudly to our children, to our parents, to our peers. Each one of us is witnessing by his life to those around. What are we saying to them? Are we reflecting the joy of Jesus? Do we radiate a concern and a love for others? Are we sparking individuals to enthusiasm and inspiration? Do we provide comfort to those going through a trial?

Our schools are also doing their job of witnessing, too! The general appearance tells the children and parents a story. Do the classroom bulletin boards and general image of the room express "happy," "creative," "neat"? Or do they say "sad," "untidy," "dull"?

The school program, budget, bulletins, and so forth, all tell stories to the families of the school. What do these things say? Each person must step outside of himself and take a good look.

Ask the Holy Spirit to open your eyes and to show you what you can do to be a better witness. Share with your school officials in a positive, loving way any negative messages that seem to be flowing unconsciously from the program, building, or the office.

The challenge of the day should be to allow the Holy Spirit to do His witnessing through you . . . and through your school.

18

HE WAS THERE BEFORE....

For we have not an high priest which cannot be touched with the feeling of our infirmities; but was in all points tempted like as we are, yet without sin.

Let us therefore come boldly unto the throne of grace that we may obtain mercy, and find grace to help in time of need. *Hebrews 4:15, 16*

One of the great comforting factors of God's wonderful Word is that He has already experienced every emotional impact we have faced or will face. Even though times have changed, environments are different, and schools and programs are upon us, man's emotional faculties are the same since time began. Therefore, in spite of the fact that Jesus never went through a school board meeting, He was in situations where identical emotional energies were utilized and tested.

Throughout a "normal" school day, we move about in many directions. We go from personnel, to program, to pupil with many interpersonal feelings and reactions. We are often tempted to act irrationally or irritably. However, the Holy Spirit must control us. At times we are misunderstood. Jesus had the same problem. Lies about the Lord were spread on many occasions. He bore them in love and patience. He was accused of some of the worst sins of the day, but His life and manner proved Him faultless. Jesus knew what it was to have friends who forsook Him when He needed them most.

From the Scriptures, we learn that Jesus did meet all the emotional issues similar to those that greet us in our life and in our school work today. It is, therefore, imperative that we try to handle each case as He would. In many instances it is clear as to what He did and how He felt. In some portions it is not clear; however, we can rest assured He complied with His own spiritual laws. The commandments of the Lord must be followed under the power of the Holy Spirit. Love of God must flow through each of us to others. Negative thoughts of resentment, bitterness, jealousy, and so forth, must all give way to Philippians 4:8, "Finally, brethren, whatsoever things are true, whatsoever things are honest, whatsoever things are just, whatsoever things are pure, whatsoever things are lovely, whatsoever things are of good report; if there be any virtue, and if there be any praise, think on these things."

As we are journeying through life, and our burdens get heavy and press on our shoulders lowering our chins, we suddenly see footprints . . . the footprints of Jesus! He already has been this way before us!

As you continue to follow the footprints with your eyes, they finally disappear into the horizon. However, your heads are now higher and you can look up and fix your eyes . . . on Him!

19

AN INSTRUMENT

For while one saith, I am of Paul; and another, I am of Apollos; are ye not carnal?

Who then is Paul, and who is Apollos, but ministers by whom ye believed, even as the Lord gave to every man?

I have planted, Apollos watered; but God gave the increase.

So then neither is he that planteth any thing, neither he that watereth; but God that giveth the increase.

Now he that planteth and he that watereth are one: and every man shall receive his own reward according to his own labour. *I Corinthians 3:4-8*

The overriding motivation for each day's work in the life of the Christian educator, is being faithful and obedient to God. Each day as we face the boys and girls, we are not sure of their spiritual depth. Some, very obviously know the Lord as Saviour, and others, it is quite certain, do not. However, how about the majority? What do they all need?

From the portion of Scripture read earlier, we note that God giveth the increase. Even though we may not know what each student needs specifically, the Holy Spirit will guide to fulfill these needs in proportion as we are walking in close communion with Him.

In some cases we will be the planters of the seed. We will be the first real gospel carriers these children will be exposed to in their lives. In other instances our spiritual lessons will be like fresh rain soaking the roots of a tender plant ... water to cause that plant to grow toward full maturity.

Finally, there will be situations where we will be the harvester's blade. The one to lead that student to make his clear decision, for Christ will hopefully be his teacher.

God has His perfect timetable for our lives. The main responsibility of the educator is to be open to the leading of the Lord and allow Him to use us as the seed, the water, or the blade. In the course of the school year, it is quite possible that the teacher could be all three. He could be the one to first expose the child to the gospel; then be the one to water and nurture the Word; then, finally, to lead the student to the saving knowledge of Jesus Christ.

Therefore, it is quite evident that we must not glory in any part of the total process. We see that God is the One to receive all the glory, for we are only instruments in His hands as we are yielded to Him. It is imperative, then, that we be in perfect fellowship with the Father through prayer and study of His Word daily. Otherwise, the total work can be injured or greatly curtailed. A farmer can quickly attest to the problems that develop if the planting, watering, or harvesting processes are delayed. The end result is not what the farmer intended.

God places certain students in your classes according to His will. He knows what these students need, and He knows that you can provide these needs if you allow Him to work through you. An instrument has to be clean and available to be used, and this is what God is asking of you. Seed ... water ... or harvester's blade, what difference does it make, if God gives the increase.

20

SATAN'S CIRCUMSTANCES

And he began to teach them, that the Son of man must suffer many things, and be rejected of the elders, and of the chief priests, and scribes, and be killed, and after three days rise again.

And he spake that saying openly. And Peter took him, and began to rebuke him.

But when he had turned about and looked on his disciples, he rebuked Peter, saying, Get thee behind me, Satan: for thou savourest not the things that be of God, but the things that be of men. *Mark 8:31-33*

Jesus has just beautifully and clearly explained how His last moments on earth would pass before returning to Heaven. It was a spiritually moving time when suddenly Satan's hand of confusion, through circumstance, unfolds. Jesus identifies his attacker quickly, saying that he can influence men's work but not God's.

One of Satan's pet tricks is to ride along with a blessing from the Lord. God is about to guide and direct when Satan steps in with some physical circumstances that look good but can cause the short-circuit of God's best. Often we tend to forget that Satan can also control circumstances. I remember one occasion when a secular school teacher, with a fine testimony, felt God's leading into Christian school work. She had prayed, investigated, and was ready to take the step of faith. Before actually giving her word, however, she got two telephone calls offering her jobs in two different secular schools. She felt God had directed these calls to her to keep her in the public schools as a witness. So she accepted one of them, and the Christian school work was forgotten.

In our classrooms, we plan for certain spiritual activities only to find that often some circumstances are pulling at us to change these plans. Possibly we were planning to speak to a student or a parent about his relationship to Christ when something altered this objective. We can be sure that Satan will never stand idly by when we are about to accomplish or attempt something for the Lord. Careful planning needs to take into account that there will emerge some type of opposition for which we must be prepared. Watch and pray are good orders!

On occasion God most certainly does redirect plans and we need to be open to the Holy Spirit's leading. However, to base His leading on some changing physical circumstances can be very misleading. God has said that Satan is the prince of the power of the air. Therefore, he would be capable of manipulating events to a certain degree to gain an advantage. We need to pray fervently, plan carefully, and proceed with determination to do *His will.*

If you, as a teacher for Christ, move with this confidence, God will direct you while thwarting Satan. As blessings come . . . watch and be aware of the ways the enemy will attempt to block them.

. . . thanks be unto God which always causeth you to triumph in Christ. . . .

21

WORDS ARE INEXPENSIVE

But I have prayed for thee, that thy faith fail not: and when thou art converted, strengthen thy brethren.

And he said unto him, Lord, I am ready to go with thee, both into prison, and to death.

And he said, I tell thee, Peter, the cock shall not crow this day, before that thou shalt thrice deny that thou knowest me.

And Peter said, Man, I know not what thou sayest. And immediately, while he yet spake, the cock crew. And the Lord turned, and looked upon Peter. And Peter remembered the word of the Lord, how he had said unto him, Before the cock crow, thou shalt deny me thrice.

Luke 22:32-34, 60, 61

As Peter looked into the face of Jesus, he gave one of the most inspiring statements of love and dedication to the Lord a person could possibly give. However, Peter had a backslidden heart! He had the words, but it did not change his inner condition; he was on his way down.

So often a person's spiritual depth cannot be evaluated on his words alone. Christians, even non-Christians, can give a good word of testimony at a convenient place or at a time when an impression is desired. This is why it is so vital to have more evaluative criteria, when selecting someone for a job, than just an interview.

In Matthew 7:16-17, a check list for false teachers is given. Those that are of Christ are brought under the light of Galatians 5:22-23. Both of these portions of Scripture revolve around the truth that by their fruits we will know them... not by their words.

There are several other instances in the Bible where words of truth did not reflect the true attitudes of the heart. One was in Luke 10:25 when the lawyer answered Jesus' question and told the Lord what had to be done to inherit eternal life. Jesus then said, "You have answered right. Do it and live." The lawyer had the words, but the reality of them was lacking in his life.

In Mark 12:32-34, we read:

And the scribe said unto him, Well, Master, thou hast said the truth: for there is one God; and there is none other but he: And to love him with all the heart, and with all the understanding, and with all the soul, and with all the strength, and to love his neighbour as himself, is more than all whole burnt offerings and sacrifices. And when Jesus saw that he answered discreetly, he said unto him, Thou art not far from the kingdom of God. And no man after that durst ask him any question.

This day, weigh your words in the LIGHT of your life... not by the ELOQUENCE of your words.

22

THE HIGHEST CALLING

Be not thou therefore ashamed of the testimony of our Lord, nor of me his prisoner: but be thou partaker of the afflictions of the gospel according to the power of God;

Who hath saved us, and called us with an holy calling, not according to our works, but according to his own purpose and grace, which was given us in Christ Jesus before the world began. *II Timothy 1:8, 9*

The Office of Education and Welfare in Washington, D. C., lists in one of its catalogs 24,000 possible careers for high school and college graduates. It would be a monumental task to attempt to list these careers in order of importance. In fact, it would be nigh impossible to do so. However, as Christians, we know what job would be at the very top. Without question, there is no more vital work in all the world than dealing with men's souls. This job is number one—eternity is at stake!

What shall it profit a man if he gain the whole world and lose his own soul? (Matt. 16:26).

The second most crucial work would be dealing with men's minds: namely, the field of teaching. How could there be any other work unless there were teachers to prepare the workers? Where would doctors, lawyers, engineers, and other professionals come from unless they were taught?

It is a staggering thought to realize that the Christian educator's position actually encompasses careers number one and number two. We deal with the mind as well as the soul day after day. What an awesome responsibility! To be in our position is certainly a very high calling of God! Apart from the Lord, we can do nothing.

I can do all things through Christ which strengtheneth me (Phil. 4:13).

Each day we must evaluate clearly the importance of our work and then pray earnestly that He will give us the strength and wisdom for it. Satan will attempt to render us weak in several ways. If we are conscientious, he will prompt us to worry more about our lesson plan, marking of papers, and classroom projects rather than praying for our students and preparing ourselves spiritually.

If we tend to be easy going, he will tempt us to forget about school when we get home. He'll whisper, "You worked hard enough today, you deserve to have this evening to yourself. You'll teach better tomorrow, you won't be stale," and so forth.

Spending time planning your work is good. Taking time for rest and recreation is good, too. However, NOTHING must replace the valuable time alone with the Lord because you are one of His most precious workers. You are dealing with men's souls . . . and their minds.

23

WE HEARD HIM OURSELVES

So when the Samaritans were come unto him, they besought him that he would tarry with them: and he abode there two days.

And many more believed because of his own word;

And said unto the woman, Now we believe, not because of thy saying: for we have heard him ourselves, and know this is indeed the Christ, the Saviour of the world. *John 4:40-42*

Here was a group of Samaritans challenged to know more about Jesus Christ. Finally, it was the actual words of Jesus Himself that made them believe in Him, not the words of the woman at the well.

Each day we refer to God's Word directly and indirectly in our teaching. It becomes such a matter of fact that sometimes students get the feeling it is the teacher's word. Therefore, the objective must be to help the students keep their eyes on the Lord and His Word. "God says," "The Bible says," "God's Word tells us," and so forth, have to be used very often each day. We must direct our students to read for themselves what the Bible says.

We are aware of the Bereans' philosophy found in Acts 17:11:

These were more noble than those in Thessalonica, in that they received the word with all readiness of mind, and searched the scriptures daily, whether those things were so.

This same important challenge must be presented to our classes. It is ultimately the Word that brings men to believe, then to receive Christ, and finally to modify one's life style through the Holy Spirit's power. As the Word strengthens the spiritual growth of the teacher, so it will strengthen the spiritual growth of the children. The earlier the children experience the Word's power, the sooner they will mature in Him.

When the woman at the well was convinced Jesus was the Messiah, and received joyfully His Word, it states she left her waterpot and ran to the village. Why would she abandon the waterpot and this very valuable water? Why not? For now she has the whole well in her heart!

You must work toward making your children strong enough to stand on their own spiritual legs; to drink from their heart-well, supplied by God Himself. Be creative in designing assignments to cause your students to dig into God's Word for themselves. Many adults today are still spiritual babes because they can't feed themselves. They have not been taught or challenged enough to do so. As a Christian educator you have the best opportunities to do this early in the child's life. Do not miss these precious moments to excite and encourage your students to see what wonderful promises and provisions our loving God has for them. The most effective way this can be done is to tell the students what YOU have learned from Him . . . today!

24

DOWNWARD PULL

I beseech you therefore, brethren, by the mercies of God, that ye present your bodies a living sacrifice, holy, acceptable unto God, which is your reasonable service.

And be not conformed to this world: but be ye transformed by the renewing of your mind, that ye may prove what is that good, and acceptable, and perfect, will of God.
Romans 12:1-2

But put ye on the Lord Jesus Christ, and make not provision for the flesh, to fulfil the lusts thereof. *Romans 13:14*

As Christians, each of us feels the downward pull of the world, the flesh, and the devil each day. All of these forces are working on us, trying to twist us into some compromise. If we do yield, we find the compromise has no end, but sinks continually to lower levels. There is no let-up! However, we can thank God that through Jesus Christ and His Word, we can do all things. God can establish the standards in our lives and give us the strength to maintain them.

In the classroom the downward pull continues in a different way. As teachers we organize our goals and objectives spiritually, academically, and socially, only to find there is a continual battle to keep them high. There is an unorganized attempt to make us compromise day after day. Students forget to be courteous. They talk when they should work; they speak while others speak; they push and shove their way to and through doorways; the list is endless. We rationalize that this is a "new breed" of student that needs more freedom, so we compromise and tolerate this impudent behavior.

Spiritually, the students question the basic truths of the Bible, they rebel against authority, and their attitudes tend to dampen the enthusiasm of others for Christ. Generally they are spiritual sluggards. We, in turn, concede they have a good point and so become less forceful in our teaching; we soften our approach in reaching others for Christ.

Academically, assignments come in late or in poor form; work projects are curtailed due to "class static"; pressure to ease up grading procedures becomes acute. The downward pull begins its work and we slowly gravitate to the level of the class.

The Bible warns against giving in to the flesh or taking the path of least resistance. Only the mediocre teacher is satisfied with his performance each day. All others are continually striving for greater success.

You need to pray, plan, and set high (but reachable) goals and stick to them. With love, prayer, and hard work, you must labor with each student to motivate him to reach those goals. He'll admire you after the semester dust settles. What is more important, he will be on a higher level of thinking and will be on his way to greater, more effective service for Jesus Christ.

Don't give in . . . or up . . . give out!

25

GOD DID IT

Therefore his sisters sent unto him, saying, Lord, behold, he whom thou lovest is sick.

When Jesus heard that, he said, This sickness is not unto death, but for the glory of God, that the Son of God might be glorified thereby.

Now Jesus loved Martha, and her sister, and Lazarus.

When he had heard therefore that he was sick, he abode two days still in the same place where he was.

Then said Jesus unto them plainly, Lazarus is dead.

And I am glad for your sakes that I was not there, to the intent ye may believe; nevertheless let us go unto him.
John 11:3-6, 14, 15

After Jesus hears that His very close friend, Lazarus, is sick, He does not immediately respond, but waits two more days. Why does the Lord procrastinate in this manner when every available minute counts for life?

At times we also ask the Lord the same question in the midst of a trying situation. We want the hand of God to move quickly. We pray. We cry. We yearn for an answer. But all is silent! At the proper moment, the Lord responds and we recognize the fact . . . His timing is best!

In John 11:15, we learn why Jesus waited before seeing Lazarus and why He waits in many other such cases. Jesus says, "I am glad for your sakes that I was not there, *to the intent ye may believe;* nevertheless, let us go unto him."

If Jesus had ministered earlier to Lazarus, people would have felt that Lazarus was going to recuperate anyway. Possibly, he was not that sick! Since Jesus waited and Lazarus died, there was no doubt in anyone's mind of the true situation. Everything rested with God! When the miracle was performed, they all knew it was God who did it.

Often when answers come quickly to prayers, we forget God answered! We feel that things would probably have straightened out anyway with a little more time. However, in some cases, He allows the situation to go so far that there is no doubt in anyone's mind that only God is going to be able to intervene and provide the solution.

God knows our human frame too well. We do not acknowledge or glorify God enough. We are too quick to justify ourselves and our efforts even though they may have a good spiritual base. The Lord in His mercy loves us and desires our love and attention at all times.

In your life and in the life of your school, He allows things to develop where you have no other recourse than to turn everything over to Him. See His loving hand perform the miracle and then you can say . . . "He did it all!"

Pray, persevere . . . wait, receive . . . that without question you may believe!

26

COMPLETENESS IN CHRIST

Beware lest any man spoil you though philosophy and vain deceit, after the tradition of men, after the rudiments of the world, and not after Christ.

For in him dwelleth all the fulness of the Godhead bodily.

And ye are complete in him, which is the head of all principality and power. *Colossians 2:8-10*

Nearly everyone concerned about nutrition knows there are seven basic foods that need to be eaten consistently if man is to be physically healthy. However, for good mental health, many do not realize there are seven other vital needs. As Christian educators we need to be very aware of these psychological needs so that we can adequately minister to our classes. Spending hours and hours on math, science, and other academic skills may not be meeting the most important needs of some of our students. It appears that poor mental health is rapidly increasing, causing extensive academic as well as other types of damage. Serious mental illness among adults is also alarmingly on the upswing.

If the seven basic psychological needs are not being met, then there are bound to be some emotional "hang-ups" developing. What are these critical needs? The two most important are that *man needs to be loved*, and in turn *needs to love*. He also needs *recognition*, *security*, a *purpose in life*, *periodic achievement*, and *freedom from guilt complexes*. In Colossians 2:10, we read that ". . . ye are complete in him which is the head of all principality and power."

Is it possible that a person *can* be complete in Christ? Can the Lord make up deficiencies that exist within the mental and emotional framework of an individual? The answer according to God is yes! John 3:16 and I John 4:9 are two of many verses indicating God's great, unsearchable love of man. If each person could only know a true portion of this love! So often we sing about this love, talk about God's love, read about this love, and still do not really know His love in a personal way. We must pray that we may grow in understanding and appreciation of this love.

If we truly take hold of God's love, and His love truly takes hold of us, then we can adequately love others. I John 4:7 commands us to do it! However, knowing how to love others and actually being able to love are two different things. We must tell the Lord how much we love Him, trust Him fully, yield to the Holy Spirit, read His Word and meditate on key love verses, and then allow ourselves to be open and sensitive to others' needs. We then move out to love others and win them to Christ! We have the power of supernatural love, the ability to love the unlovely as well as the lovely, when we know and love Jesus Christ personally.

Recognition is important to good mental health . . . having others know us and know we exist. What greater recognition can we have than to know the Son of God recognizes us! As Saviour, He is our constant companion recognizing us every moment of each day In fact, His Word promises not only to keep us and not forsake us, but work out all things together for our good (Rom. 8:28).

> And I give unto them eternal life; and they shall never perish, neither shall any man pluck them out of my hand. My Father, which gave them me, is greater than all; and no man is able to pluck them out of my Father's hand (John 10:28, 29).

Someone said that no one can pluck us out of God's hand, but we may slip out! It is impossible to slip out when God is holding our hand! What security this is to the believer in Christ when most of the world cringes in insecurity every day!

A purpose in life is the great motivator for each of us. When a purpose is lacking, internal problems will develop. The child of God will not lack a purpose when he knows and heeds God's Word. First, we are becoming conformed to the image of Christ as we allow the Holy Spirit to shape us (Rom. 8:29). Second, Mark 16:15 gives us our world-wide commission. It states, ". . . go ye into all the world, and preach the gospel to every creature."

Daniel tells us that "he that winneth souls is wise" (Dan. 12:3). He says this not only because the soulwinner is going to have great rewards in heaven, but also because that person has a "glowing," "going" inner force that gives him great daily drive. If, as Christians we are not desirous of personally changing to become like Christ or concerned actively to win others to the Lord, we are inviting internal spiritual problems.

As we strive toward these goals, we must see periodic achievements or the sense of failure overtakes us. If we labor in prayer and through love, God will reward us. Galatians 5:22, 23 outlines the fruits of the Spirit and as we yield to the Holy Spirit, we see these fruits develop within us.

An ill-tempered man must allow the Lord to control his irritation. In fact, he should thank God for each trying situation, realizing there is a lesson for him in this trial of patience; longsuffering, he starts to mature. Peace, gentleness, joy, and all the other fruits start growing, in accordance with his yieldedness to the Holy Spirit, thus blessing and motivating him.

In soulwinning, as we seek to witness and win souls to Christ, we are promised success in this endeavor (Ps. 2:8). As we lead one soul to the Lord, what a joy, blessing, and encouragement it can be to lead others also to the Saviour!

If one common trait appears, as a consistent pattern in those having emotional problems, it is that a keen sense of guilt is present. So many have guilt complexes. The reason this is true is that we are all guilty! (Rom. 3:23). Again, Jesus Christ can remove this guilt by forgiving sins, both in the Christian (I John 1:9) and in the unsaved (Eph. 1:7). No one, therefore, needs to be under the strain of guilt.

Jesus Christ *can* meet all of the psychological needs of men. Therefore, we *can* be complete in Him.

As an educator, you must be certain you are complete (mature) in Him and work with your students to see that they, too, are complete in Christ.

27
SECULAR EDUCATION ...
OFFENSE ... OR AN OFFENSE

And they brought young children to him, that he should touch them: and his disciples rebuked those that brought them.

But when Jesus saw it, he was much displeased, and said unto them, Suffer the little children to come unto me, and forbid them not: for of such is the kingdom of God.

Verily I say unto you, Whosoever shall not receive the kingdom of God as a little child, he shall not enter therein.

And he took them up in his arms, put his hands upon them, and blessed them. *Mark 10:13-16*

And whosoever shall offend one of these little ones that believe in me, it is better for him that a millstone were hanged about his neck, and he were cast into the sea. *Mark 9:42*

So often well-meaning Christians like to uphold secular education by saying that it is preparing their child to face the world. They feel that this education is a vital tool to keep their child on the offensive as they cope with the winds of adversity. Little do these parents realize that secular education is actually an offense to the child and it is in reality working to make him conform to the world.

John 14:6 states the actual words of Jesus as "I am the way, the truth, and the life. . . ."

If a school is not taking its students the way of Jesus Christ, the school is leading the children astray. The Lord didn't state that His way was "a way" or "some way" but "the way." This leaves no other possibility. There is only one right way! The wrong way is an offense to any child.

Jesus says that He is *the truth.* Any statement like that means that all other truth must begin and end with Jesus Christ and if it does not, then it is not truth. It may be a fact of this world, but not enduring truth. If a school is not resting on Jesus Christ, then it is not founded on truth. A school not secure on truth is an offense to all children.

In Christ is *life!* To prepare a girl or boy to face life without the author and sustainer of life is foolishness. God created the earth and all things on the earth, including each one of us. The Creator knows His creation and His creatures. For a school to be training students in the arts and sciences for the purpose of being helpful to society is one of the highest goals of education. To attempt to do this without the One who created all things and Who is our daily resource, is sheer folly. To discuss the world and its contents without discussing the Creator, is an offense to children. Children are not to be shielded from the truth they need to know.

Ephesians 6:4 states "... fathers, provoke not your children to wrath: but bring them up in the nurture and admonition of the Lord."

Teachers replace parents during the day. They are to bring up these children in the love and correction of the Lord.

Teachers, if you do not do this, you become an offense to the student, provoking him to false ways, false values, and a false view of life ... the greatest of all offenses to a child.

Christian education is a student's best offense ... will you prepare him well?

28

BEING A POWERFUL SERVANT

For the kingdom of God is not in word, but in power.
I Corinthians 4:20

For the preaching of the cross is to them that perish foolishness; but unto us which are saved it is the power of God.
I Corinthians 1:18

Are you a powerful servant for the Lord in your daily work? It is quite evident from our first portion of Scripture that the kingdom of God is to be of *power*. Power means we make things happen for the glory of God. Each day in our schools we all face situations that need powerful direction or powerful solutions. What is the secret of the power of God?

In our second portion of His Word we see clearly the answer to securing power. It comes through the preaching of the cross. We need to be totally involved in the preaching of the cross of Jesus Christ every single day. First of all, our own eternal lives were brought into reality by this precious sacrifice of Christ on the cross. Then this same act of love must be broadcast to the ends of the earth by each child of His. We need to cultivate daily a natural outflow of witness to our peers, pupils, and parents. There must be no exception!

To teach the Bible daily in a routine way nets routine results. Teaching with enthusiasm, joy, and a spirit of expectancy nets inspiration, gladness, and a desire for more. The cross must be central in our theme. Dates and chronologies have their place, but power comes from *the preaching of the cross.*

Each staff member of a Christian School must be a *consistent* "soulwinner." He must be vigilant to lead a lost person to a saving knowledge of Jesus Christ. To have a sensitive spirit toward others in regard to their spiritual welfare is developed by prayer and a desire to share the cross. "Ye have not because ye ask not." Have you honestly asked the Lord to lay individuals on your heart to lead them to Christ? Has God denied you souls?

If you are willing to allow the Lord to speak through your tongue, you pray specifically and watch Him open opportunity after opportunity. Then as you preach the cross, you become more powerful and you see things happen. At this point, you realize your total dependence is upon Him, so you go back to His Word and pray more. What a beautiful cycle develops.

For the preaching of the cross is the power of God!

29

JESUS ... EMPLOYED IN YOUR SCHOOL

I am crucified with Christ; nevertheless I live; yet not I, but Christ liveth in me: and the life which I now live in the flesh I live by the faith of the Son of God, who loved me, and gave himself for me. *Galatians 2:20*

Suppose it were possible that Jesus Christ could be physically involved with your school. In what capacity would He function? Due to His infinite wisdom and understanding would He choose to be Chairman of your Board? He would know the end from the beginning and would, therefore, make all the proper decisions. This in turn could lead to a more effective program, and that would certainly net many, many more students to be trained for His glory. Board meetings would progress smoothly because everyone would abide by His Word. Being in the presence of His Holy Spirit, each person would control his words and thoughts. Each one would esteem others better than himself. No man would insist on his own way. The atmosphere would be one of cordiality and cooperation. Things would be accomplished; the school would move forward ... if Jesus were on the Board. He *is* present at board meetings!

Since He was the leader of His disciples and knew how to challenge and motivate men, would it not be natural for Him to be the Headmaster of the school? In this capacity, He would gently speak and guide His staff. Teachers would respond to this sincere, loving counsel. Rules and regulations designed for staff or students would be accepted and heeded accordingly. He *does* expect us to follow rules!

Of course, all of mankind knows Him as the Master Teacher, teaching the most profound truths clearly and effectively day after day. Captivating large audiences with His magnetic love and divine sensitivity is a simple task for Jesus. The children would see Jesus in front of the classroom and love Him. They would be motivated to learn. Because they are children, there would be the daily moments of foolishness and carelessness, but as corrected by His Holy Spirit, they would respond. He *does* observe classrooms every day!

Is it possible that due to great humility He would choose to take, in your school, a much lesser position like the bus driver, the secretary, or the custodian? Would He choose one of those jobs to be an example? He *does* work with the nonteaching staff each day!

It is not a hypothetical situation, Jesus IS directly involved with your school, and He has chosen the position He will fill. He will take the job YOU are doing and will do the job through YOU... as YOU allow Him.

To whom God would make known what is the riches of the glory of this mystery among the Gentiles; which is Christ in you, the hope of glory;

Whereunto I also labour, striving according to His working, which worketh in me mightily.   *Colossians 1:27, 29*

Christ wants to do a mighty work through you and your position at the school. Why not yield to the Holy Spirit and let Him?

30

PROBLEMS TEACH LESSONS

My brethren count it all joy when ye fall into divers temptations (trials); knowing this that the trying of your faith worketh patience. But let patience have her perfect work, that ye may be perfect and entire, wanting nothing.
James 1:2-4

"How are things going at the school?"

I'm sure the question is directed to you many, many times each year. If you are like me, you say, "Fine," thinking of the ways the Lord is blessing you, but at the same time feeling a little hypocritical, knowing that you do have some problems. What kind of answer does God expect you to give to this question?

God is not interested in our explanations as much as He is interested in our attitudes! I Thessalonians 5:18 states, ". . . in everything give thanks: for this is the will of God in Christ Jesus concerning you."

To have problems is normal, especially for a Christ-centered work like ours. If we have caused these problems, God will teach us lessons through them, if we are willing to learn. If the problems are not our fault, but we respond with good Christian principles and procedures, we will be strengthened and prepared for bigger battles ahead. In either case, thank the Lord for His love which covers and guides us.

Cultivate a spirit of gratefulness . . . in all things!

Respect and welcome your problems . . . you learn from them.

31

GIVE NO OFFENSE

We, then, as workers together with him, beseech you also that ye receive not the grace of God in vain.

Giving no offense in any thing, that the ministry be not blamed.

But in all things approving ourselves as the ministers of God, in much patience, in afflictions, in necessities, in distresses,

In stripes, in imprisonments, in tumults, in labours, in watchings, in fastings; *II Corinthians 6:1, 3-5*

If the Apostle Paul were living on earth today, we certainly could say as Christian educators that we are workers together with him. We do have a vital ministry and are, therefore, ministers of God. Often we find ourselves in teaching routines day in and day out, and the keen edge of our work becomes dulled. The importance of our position, if it were felt at all, fades rapidly. We just do not realize the far-reaching influence of our jobs! We tend to live no higher than the "average" Christian in the "average" fundamental church. Whereas, we should be walking like the Minister of an "on fire" sound fundamental church with a high regard for our testimony before others.

We are ministering academically and spiritually to a congregation of about 25 students daily. (This is, in fact, larger than a number of churches across this world.) This responsibility calls for the highest degree of care and effort. We must not give offense in anything. Our talk in the classroom, our walk through the school, our life in the community, must all be conducted as though everyone were watching us. This means we are going to weigh our actions and words carefully before the Lord before we proceed in every instance. Wouldn't we do that if we were a minister of a large church? Is being the minister of a classroom different, since we are also dealing with souls? Does this give us the right to be loose and careless as Christian teachers? I do not think so, and I do not believe you do, either.

We are nonchalant because generally we think our work is not crucial before the Lord. The devil has gotten us to focus on the fact that there are millions of teachers in this world and we are "just one of them." One of the critical missions of Satan is to reduce our importance in our own eyes and before the Lord. If he succeeds, it opens the way to a casual behavior in our schools that in turn diminishes our effectiveness as spiritual leaders.

Take a moment to read the verses again in the beginning. Note that the ministry, our work, is to be highly regarded, and we are not to cast shame on it by giving offense to anyone. We must be willing and eager to give up that sin or thing which is a stumbling block of some type. To illustrate: When my church membership was becoming a problem to a number of parents in our school, I weighed the situation carefully and realized they had a good point. Although I had a good point, too, I felt for the unity of the school and the sake of the ministry, I should withdraw my membership after being part of that church for ten years. It was not a happy decision for my family, but a necessary one for the continuance of the work of Christ in our school.

How important is God's work in your school, to you . . . enough to reevaluate your total testimony before others?

Your best defense . . . is no offense!

32

THE DISCIPLE OF CHRIST

Then said Jesus to those Jews which believed on him, If ye continue in my word, then are ye my disciples indeed.
John 8:31

A new commandment I give unto you, That ye love one another; as I have loved you, that ye also love one another.

By this shall all men know that ye are my disciples, if ye have love one to another. *John 13:34, 35*

In discussing the qualities of a master teacher, there are many aspects that must be considered. The same applies as one deliberates upon discipleship traits. However, there are two key qualities the disciple (or teacher) must have as given directly by Jesus. First, he must continue in God's Word. One day a Christian friend of mine was greatly challenged and moved by a question. The question posed to him was, "What are you doing to master the Word of God?"

As I heard this, I, too, was stirred to evaluate my devotional life. However, a greater thought struck me later. What am I doing to let the Word of God master me?

As Christians, we hear so many excellent messages, we read great Christian literature; the Bible's truths coming directly and indirectly at us all the time have given us a great reservoir of Bible knowledge. So the main problem is not that we do not know enough, but that these truths have not all found themselves fully working in our lives. James tells us that we are to be doers of the Word. As we hear or read a striking truth, we need to write it down immediately in our heart (not our head); pray at once and put the truth into action as soon as possible and then *continue* in His Word. Jesus said if we continue in His Word *(continue to do His will)* we are His disciples indeed!

The second chief quality of the disciple (or teacher) is to exhibit the love of God. This is closely linked with the first requirement, letting the Word master us. There are portions of Scripture that say: pray for others, including your enemies; esteem others better than yourself; give your substance to the poor; aid the widows and orphans; support the brother who has fallen; and many other "action-packed" verses. As we yield to these truths and allow them to direct us, God's love is then flowing through us.

As we work in our schools and classrooms each day, we see faces of our peers and pupils. God tells us for effectiveness, as a disciple, we must continue in His Word, having love for one another. If we want to go through the dry mechanics of our job with "mental know-how," we can do it as God gives us breath. If, on the other hand, we want to be considered disciples and to have God's full blessing, we must then by all means follow His instruction. If we are to continue in His Word, showing His love, why should we settle for anything less each day?

One day a little boy selling apples at a railroad depot had his stand knocked over by a rushing crowd. No one took time to help this lad collect and put things together. Finally, one man stopped and took time to comfort him and help him put up the apples. After everything was back to normal and the man was ready to leave, the little fellow looked up into his face and asked, "Mister, are you Jesus?"

Here was true faith in God and the love of Jesus in action in the lives of two saints of God; one a small boy selling apples, but a growing saint! In our classes we also have growing saints, developing in faith through Jesus' love in similar ways.

Let His Word hold you ... and His love mold you!

33

THE FIELDS ARE READY NOW!

Say not ye, There are yet four months, and then cometh harvest? Behold, I say unto you, Lift up your eyes, and look on the fields; for they are white already to harvest.

And he that reapeth receiveth wages, and gathereth fruit unto life eternal; that both he that soweth and he that reapeth may rejoice together. *John 4:35-36*

Someone has very aptly said that God wants us to concentrate on the present while Satan centers on the past or the future. If our thoughts can dwell on the past long enough, we become depressed and discouraged because we see our faults, mistakes, or deficiencies recurring over and over. Then again, if the future captures our attention for too lengthy a time, we become nervous and fretful with anxiety. Many individuals never have a chance to employ or to enjoy the present effectively. They are thinking about yesterday or last week or they are thinking about tonight and tomorrow. School work can also take a similar pattern.

Teachers need to be concerned about their children *now* . . . at the moment they are together in the classroom. Some teachers moan over what their students did not get last year or the year before. They are constantly complaining about how poorly their class is prepared and how much work they have missed. On the other hand, others are fearful of the future, so all their concern is centered on preparing them for the next grade. They are nervous all year thinking about what future teachers may say about them!

Our portion of Scripture challenges us to lift up our eyes because our classes are ready to be taught *now!* We need to know our children and enjoy their strengths *now.* Our skills to detect weaknesses and work with them have to be exercised *now.* Golden opportunities to lead boys and girls to Jesus Christ are presented each day. If we are living mentally in the past or future, only the most mundane periods of work or thought will eclipse what could have been the truly precious times.

There are several places where Jesus passed by only once in His earthly travels. He gave of Himself totally while He was there, knowing He would not be back. If the people did not accept Him or His teaching, at least He knew they had been given an opportunity. Our students usually pass our way only once, so we need to be ready to give ourselves to them completely.

God has ordered your steps ... and your stops. He wants you to be alert NOW to ministering to the needs of your children. He has the future in HIS hands and will lead you through when you arrive there. In the meantime, you are to lift up your eyes to the fields of the present ... where you, time, and opportunity meet for but a moment.

34

TRUE LOVE IN SCHOOL

(A Paraphrase of I Corinthians 13)

Though I speak each day and intensely love teaching, but have not *love*, I am become as sounding brass or a tinkling cymbal.

And though I have the gift of organization, and understand all educational philosophies, and all knowledge; and though I have all faith, so that I could remove the mountains of daily problems, and have not love, I am nothing.

And though I give my time and talents to help the poor new students, and though I skip lunch to do extra work, and have not love, it profiteth me nothing.

Love endures a lot, and is kind; love is not jealous of another teacher or school; love doesn't step on someone else because he disagrees; is not puffed up with a feeling of importance;

Does not act quickly in an unChristian-like way, seeketh not his own way; is not easily irritated; doesn't feel someone is always talking about him wrongly;

Doesn't rejoice when an unfriendly co-worker encounters a serious problem, but rejoices in truth.

Pray for all things; believe all things will work out, have hope in all things for the future, endure all things each day.

Love never faileth; but whether there be programs, they shall fail; whether there be new buildings, they shall crumble; whether there be knowledge, it will become outdated;

We know part of the picture now, and we can do what we can.

But when that which is perfect is come, then that which is imperfect can be done away with,

When I took over as a new teacher, I spoke as a new teacher; I understood as a new teacher; I thought as a new teacher; but when I matured a little with experience, I put away my immature actions.

I don't understand everything now, but I will someday; presently, I know a little, but there's a time coming when I'll know . . . as I am known.

And now abideth faith, hope, love, these three, but the greatest of these is love . . . your love!

35

IS A CHILD WORTH IT?

He spake also this parable; A certain man had a fig tree planted in his vineyard; and he came and sought fruit thereon, and found none.

Then said he unto the dresser of his vineyard, Behold, these three years I come seeking fruit on this fig tree, and find none; cut it down, why cumbereth it the ground?

And he answering said unto him, Lord, let it alone this year also, till I shall dig around it, and dung it:

And if it bear fruit, well: and if not, then after that thou shalt cut it down. *Luke 13:6-9*

One of my duties as a public school teacher was, of course, to attend teachers' meetings. I remember one meeting in which the principal was asking if we would like to see our class sizes reduced by three students. One teacher came out with a classic question. She asked, "Which three?" After the laughter died down, the question lingered in my mind.

So often we feel that if we could get rid of two or three in our class what a nice class it would be. We so often forget that God arranges all class rosters. He knows the kinds of students that need certain teachers. He also knows the teacher well enough to prescribe certain students for her welfare. Why then should we seek the easy way out as did the owner of the fig tree? His suggestion was to cut the tree down and clear the soil. Why let something unprofitable stay and take up space? The dresser of the vineyard realized he had not taken care of the tree properly. He wanted another chance to do it right. He would dig around it and dung it and give it the care it should have had earlier.

The digging and dunging are the symbols for work. Before we consider eliminating, or harbor the desire for eliminating any pupil from our class, we should ask ourselves whether we have given the proper amount of prayer and labor. At times a teacher will say, "I've done all I can for the boy." That teacher should have said, "I've done everything I can to him!" When you ask exactly what was done, a list of punitive measures is related. Trying one form of punishment after another is in itself no stimulus to improvement. Poor behavior must be punished, but positive constructive work must be invested in the child. Has there been personal, fervent prayer with the child and for the child? Has his home been visited? Has a conference been held with both the father and mother? Has the Pastor been contacted? Have the child's study habits been reviewed? Have his former academic skills been evaluated, and so forth?

Each class is loaded with children with great potential. We must pray for wisdom and be so open to the Holy Spirit that God's love can flow through us to all. We must be willing to work with some without counting the hours. Often someone will ask, "Is it fair to the other children to take this kind of time with one?" The answer is in God's hand. As you honestly seek the Lord, He will direct. In some cases, you will see that God wants much time invested in a certain student and in other cases not. When the answer is negative another situation will be used of God to further His program for the child. Simply, because the school is through with a student, does not mean God is through with him, too.

You have one chance with each child. Covenant before the Lord to labor diligently to do your best for him . . . the way God gives of Himself to you. . . .

36

KEEPING THE JOY

If ye keep my commandments, ye shall abide in my love; even as I have kept my Father's commandments, and abide in his love.

These things have I spoken unto you, that my joy might remain in you, and that your joy might be full.

This is my commandment, That ye love one another, as I have loved you. *John 15:10-12*

Often we hear fellow Christians and even ourselves talk about the joy that is exhibited by a new convert to Christ. We almost yearn to have that type of joy once again. Is it normal to have the joy and then lose it? According to God's Word it is not! In verse eleven of John 15, we read that Jesus wants His joy to *remain* in us and that our joy might be full.

The prerequisites to keeping the joy are found in verse ten which states, "If ye keep my commandments, ye shall abide in my love...."

The reason we lose the joy is that we do not continue to follow His commandments. We would not think of violating God's Word about some things, but yet in other areas we are lax.

Let us examine a series of directives from the Lord:

(1) Let not the sun go down upon your wrath (Eph. 4:26).

(2) Let him that stole steal no more (Eph. 4:28).

(3) Let no corrupt communication proceed out of your mouth (Eph. 4:29).

(4) Let all bitterness and wrath and anger and clamour and evil speaking, be put away from you (Eph. 4:31).

(5) Be ye kind one to another, tenderhearted, forgiving one another (Eph. 4:32).

(6) Let nothing be done through strife or vainglory (Phil. 2:3).

(7) Do all things without murmurings and disputings (Phil. 2:14).

(8) Rejoice in the Lord alway (Phil. 4:4).

(9) Whatsoever things are true, whatsoever things are honest, whatsoever things are just, whatsoever things are pure, whatsoever things are lovely, whatsoever things are of good report; if there be any virtue, and if there be any praise, think on these things (Phil. 4:8).

Are you faithfully complying with all of these directives? Maybe the joy level is regulated by the obedience level. According to the Word, this is most certainly the case; obedience begets joy.

Do not tolerate weaknesses in your life. They will sap your joy resources. Confess each area where you are deficient. Pray and work to be sure you are obeying each commandment completely. Watch your joy return and fill you. Spread a little joy in your own heart, and then around the school today. Joy is very infectious and it can make you a better communicator. Rejoice in the Lord!

37

ONE PAIR OF EYES

And I say unto you my friends, Be not afraid of them that kill the body, and after that have no more that they can do.

But I will forewarn you whom ye shall fear: Fear him, which after he hath killed hath power to cast into hell; yea, I say unto you, Fear him. *Luke 12:4-5*

A professional football player was asked one time what he thought about when he was in a big game with about seventy thousand pairs of eyes watching him. His answer was quite unusual. He said that out of all those eyes, he was concerned about only one pair . . . those of his coach. It did not matter what anyone in the stadium was thinking about, but it did matter what his coach thought. If everyone cheered and praised him, yet his coach felt he had failed . . . he failed!

In Ephesians 6:6-7, it states:

Not with eyeservice, as menpleasers; but as the servants of Christ, doing the will of God from the heart; With good will doing service, as to the Lord, and not to men.

Each day we perform before many; our students, fellow staff members, supervisors, parents, and school board members. Whose eyes are we concerned about? Whom are we trying to please? As redeemed men and women, we really have no choice. We must please Him, who has called us to eternal life. If we find ourselves in the fleshly pattern of thinking more about pleasing people in order to hold our jobs or to push ahead, our efforts will all be in the flesh and not in the Spirit.

In desiring to please the Lord, we must realize certain points. God has decreed that there are chains of command in the lives of each of us and we are to submit to these in authority over us. The Lord does not give direct orders to His servants that run cross-current to the rules of the school authorities. God will work through those whom He has placed at the helm. There may come a time when He may remove them . . . or you.

Therefore, day by day as you labor in love while working with children, you must keep your eyes fixed on Christ. Strive to please Him in all that you do. When the cheers and accolades of men have subsided, the question will be, what did the Lord think of your service today?

Yes, I'm satisfied with Jesus, He's done so much for me,

But the most important question . . . is Jesus satisfied with me?

38

GAINING EXPERIENCE . . . HOPE

My brethren, count it all joy when ye fall into divers temptations;

Knowing this, that the trying of your faith worketh patience.

But let patience have her perfect work, that ye may be perfect and entire, wanting nothing. *James 1:2-4*

And not only so, but we glory in tribulations also: knowing that tribulation worketh patience;

And patience, experience; and experience, hope:

And hope maketh not ashamed; because the love of God is shed abroad in our hearts by the Holy Ghost which is given unto us. *Romans 5:3-5*

Some Christian teachers have a number of years of experience, while others have one year of experience a number of times! What a difference! From the two portions of Scripture, several vital points are noted. Tribulations work our patience and patience develops experience. Will this work automatically? No! The key to this part of the picture is whether or not we are glorying in our tribulations. Glorying means we are accepting the daily problems and trials, and counting it joy as James tells us to do. If we are not, then we are "chafing at the bit" and thwarting the purpose of God to teach us certain lessons to develop our patience and experience. We must respond properly to every problem. There are never accidents in a child of God's life . . . only incidents! I Thessalonians 5:18 states, "in everything give thanks: for this is the will of God in Christ Jesus concerning you." In another portion of Scripture, it tells us plainly that, "all things are for your sakes." James goes so far as to say that we should treat the trials that come upon us as friends! It is through these friends (trials) that God prepares us to face and cope with the bigger and more complex problems to come.

As we continue each day to pray for wisdom, thank God for each trial that comes. Work diligently in Christian love and study the Scriptures to solve the problems. God strengthens and expands our patience . . . experience . . . hope! This broader hope within us enables us to minister to more children, more parents, and more of our co-workers. We become servants that are more experienced and mature. Five years after we started teaching, God is not still trying to teach us the little lessons He had for us the very first year.

If there seems to be a recurring problem in your life or in your classroom, you must search deeply to see if there is an unlearned lesson. As a teacher, you know that drill is still one of the best teaching tools. God, being the Master Teacher, also uses the drill lesson. He comes back to you again and again until you learn. Some disciplinary action may be needed.

Pray often that you will learn the lessons God wants to teach you the very first time . . . so you can build experience . . . hope!

39

TWO WENT UP TO PRAY

And he spake this parable unto certain which trusted in themselves that they were righteous, and despised others:

Two men went up into the temple to pray; the one a Pharisee, and the other a publican.

The Pharisee stood and prayed thus unto himself, God, I thank thee, that I am not as other men are, extortioners, unjust, adjulterers, or even as this publican.

I fast twice in the week, I give tithes of all that I possess.

And the publican, standing afar off, would not lift up so much as his eyes unto heaven, but smote upon his breast, saying, God be merciful to me a sinner.

I tell you, this man went down to his house justified rather than the other: for every one that exalteth himself shall be abased; and he that humbleth himself shall be exalted.

Luke 18:9-14

Two teachers went into the church to pray: the one, teacher of Christian School A, and the other, teacher of Christian School B.

Teacher A stood and prayed thus with himself, "God, I thank thee that I am not as other teachers who are narrow and compromising, money and power hungry, untrained, unspiritual, or even as Teacher B here. I fast twice a week, pray many times, and never mention my problems. I don't do anything that is not scriptural."

And Teacher B standing afar off, would not lift up so much as his eyes unto heaven; but smote upon his breast saying, "God help me in my weakness. Lord, you know our problems; the money we need, the students who are rebelling in their hearts against you, those others who are still not saved, and our curriculum needs continuous revision! Lord, only you can give us the victory through Christ!

I tell you, this man went to his school justified rather than the other: for every one that exalteth himself shall be abased; and he that humbleth himself shall be exalted.

We need to beware of the boasting spirit. It is so easy to compare our school with another Christian school and be quick to point out in what areas we are better. We need to strive for excellence daily but not at the expense of others.

Peter boasted of his devotion to Christ even to the point that he would follow Jesus to the death. Before the day was over Peter had denied Christ three times (Luke 22:33, 34). All trials and testings are of the Lord. James says *we* are to welcome them as friends because they will strengthen us if we face them, pray, confess and work. A boasting or self-righteous attitude has no place in the Christian school.

You need to always be positive and praising in your daily school work for the Lord. Always give God the glory each time you gain a blessing or a victory. God's hand is upon every Christ-centered school. Therefore, join hands and uphold each other before the Lord.

Help your school today ... by praying for others.

40

HOW TO PRAY FOR OTHERS

And the Lord said, Simon, Simon, behold, Satan hath desired to have you, that he may sift you as wheat:

But I have prayed for thee, that thy faith fail not: and when thou art converted, strengthen thy brethren.

And he said unto him, Lord, I am ready to go with thee, both into prison, and to death.

And he said, I tell thee, Peter, the cock shall not crow this day, before that thou shalt thrice deny that thou knowest me. *Luke 22:31-34*

So often we are challenged to pray for one another and for our students. We certainly are to follow the mandate of the Bible to "pray without ceasing." However, we are not always sure how to pray for others. Sometimes we doubt if our prayers are being answered. We expect to see certain results and if we do not see them as we want them to be, we think our prayers are unavailing.

Jesus prayed that Peter's faith would not fail, yet in a few hours Peter had denied the Lord three times. Had Peter's faith failed?

As a follower of Jesus, Peter's faith was still as an infant, and as a result he fell. If a little baby falls, do we state that he has failed? Peter's faith had much maturing to do, and after he was converted we see the result of his "grown" faith later on in God's Word, in answer to the Lord's prayer.

So often we pray for our pupils, but do not see quick answers, so we judge the child is not growing as a Christian or we may even doubt his salvation.

We must realize that he was a child before he was a Christian. By accepting Jesus Christ as Saviour his sins are forgiven, but his old nature is still present and struggling for dominence.

To continually badger a child by repeating that if he were a Christian, he would not do this or he would not do that only tends to weaken and possibly discourage the little faith he has. Certainly, sin has to be called sin and each misdemeanor has to be punished. However, the points to stress to the child are that a Christian should be truly sorry for his sin; he will want to confess it to God each time he falls; and he will pray and work hard not to fall again.

There is much supportive Scripture to bear out the fact that prayer must not cease for your students. If a student falls, you must act accordingly with love and discipline as needed. Feed your students on God's "bread of life" daily and pray that their faith will not fail, but will grow . . . as watered with prayer.

41

THE SELF IMAGE

Hast thou faith? Have it to thyself before God. Happy is he that condemneth not himself in that thing which he alloweth.

And he that doubteth is damned if he eat, because he eateth not of faith: for whatsoever is not of faith is sin.

Romans 14:22, 23

For as he thinketh in his heart, so is he; Eat and drink, saith he to thee; but his heart is not with thee. *Proverbs 23:7*

One of the most intense battles that rages in the life of a Christian is the war between the Holy Spirit and Satan. This war covers many battle-fronts, one being the area of the self-image. Satan is bent on convincing the believer that he is nothing; he is weak and can not ever be a strong Christian; he is a hypocrite; he is worldly; he falls far short of the mark of being the kind of Christian he ought to be. Satan wants to destroy the self-image of God's child!

The Holy Spirit also begins at the "nothing point." However, He does not dwell there. He moves from that point to encourage the believer to know that God loves him dearly and has a beautiful, purposeful plan for his life. God wants to work with the believer, to make the believer a powerful force for God's glory. The Christian's part is to just feed on God's Word, fellowship often in prayer, then yield to the Holy Spirit moment by moment every day. God will shape his life.

In the process of shaping this life, God will

chip off or sandpaper some rough edges. He may apply heat and pressure to continue his molding work. While this is going on, the Holy Spirit will often convict, but will never "nag." Satan majors in "nagging," reminding us often how weak and inadequate we are as Christians.

Why is the self-image a vital area of concern for God and Satan? The self-image is one of the factors that determines our motivation in life. If the self-image is poor, the life is never joyful or productive for God. Such a believer's life is irratic with nothing but frequent ups and downs. It is a life of indecision and weak faith. This believer cannot visualize himself doing anything big for God because he is reminded by Satan how wicked he is.

The Christian educator must have a good self-image. He must realize God's love and that He desires to do a mighty work in him as he works with his students.

However, I am not suggesting we tolerate sin in any degree. God says we are always to triumph in Christ. We must not condemn ourselves because of weak points in our lives. We face the fact there are things we must pray about honestly. There are areas where we must work harder or plan more. We need to walk closer to the Lord in love and devotion.

Accept yourself as an important person to God doing a vital work through Him for His glory.YOU BECOME WHAT YOU THINK YOU ARE!

42

GOD'S WILL

Peter therefore was kept in prison: but prayer was made without ceasing of the church unto God for him.

And when he had considered the thing, he came to the house of Mary the mother of John, whose surname was Mark; where many were gathered together praying.

And as Peter knocked at the door of the gate, a damsel came to hearken, named Rhoda.

And when she knew Peter's voice, she opened not the gate for gladness, but ran in, and told how Peter stood before the gate.

And they said unto her, Thou art mad. But she constantly affirmed that it was even so. Then said they, It is his angel.

But Peter continued knocking: and when they had opened the door, and saw him, they were astonished.

Acts 12:5, 12-16

This is one of the amazing accounts in God's Word in which He answered prayer almost immediately. Some believe that those gathered together in prayer lacked faith; therefore, they did not respond well when Peter was freed from prison. However, I feel that those in prayer were spiritually sound. They were not necessarily praying that Peter would be released, but that God's will would be done.

It was the Lord's desire that Peter be set free, but those in prayer did not realize this. As a result, a certain amount of time was lost until the reality of the situation gripped their aching hearts.

Often in our daily work with children and in our other general school work, we pray for God's will to be done. We know beyond a shadow of doubt that His will must be in operation or all is in vain. The beauty of buildings, books, and budgets is marred unless we are proceeding in His power and direction. However, our prayers for His will to be done do not assure us that we will recognize His will when it comes.

One of the factors that can cloud the recognition of His will is the fact that sometimes we prematurely visualize what we believe to be His will. When this happens, we are not ready for His will and His real will can be upon us without our realization. We need to pray to be ready for God's answer, whatever it may be.

We pray for more patience with our students and we visualize a great calm sweeping over us. Instead, we run head-long into chaos and a day full of turmoil. What is God's will in situations like this? His will is that we might develop patience which comes through weathering a storm. A ball player learns to play ball by being on the field; a swimmer learns to swim by being in the water; a saint learns patience by being placed in the middle of confusion.

A troublesome child or parent has us on our knees. The situation does not change, so we become frustrated. We did not see that God wanted another more creative, effective approach to the person.

There are many other situations where you want God's will in your Christian school life, but fail to fully recognize God's hand when it unfolds before you. God works best in revealing His will when you reach the moment in prayer where it does not matter what God tells you. Finally, you are willing to do whatever He wants. "Thy will be done" then has meaning. At that point, when YOUR will is out of the way, the Lord can show you clearly . . . HIS will!

43

DID YOU ASK?

Ask, and it shall be given you; seek, and ye shall find; knock, and it shall be opened unto you:

For every one that asketh receiveth; and he that seeketh findeth; and to him that knocketh it shall be opened.
Matthew 7:7, 8

If any of you lack wisdom, let him ask of God, that giveth to all men liberally, and upbraideth not; and it shall be given him.

But let him ask in faith, nothing wavering. For he that wavereth is like a wave of the sea driven with the wind and tossed. *James 1:5, 6*

Often I will say to a group that I am addressing, "How many of you ask for wisdom every day from God?" Usually two, maybe three, hands will slowly rise. Then I will follow up with the "hooker question," "How many today are wrestling with some situation that needs an important answer?" At this point nearly every hand is raised.

Isn't it strange that we do not seek wisdom from God daily, for in our classrooms we are faced with a myriad of incidents, and sometimes accidents, that need the "wisdom of Solomon"! Where did he get his wisdom? Even though he did not know brother James or what Jesus said to do, Solomon asked God directly for wisdom (I Kings 3).

And God gave Solomon wisdom and understanding exceeding much ... (I Kings 4:29).

And Solomon's wisdom excelled the wisdom of all the children of the east country and all the wisdom of Egypt (I Kings 4:30).

For he was wiser than all men (I Kings 4:31).

This same wisdom that came to Solomon from God is available to us, His chidren. However, we must ask specifically for it day by day, situation by situation without fail . . . with faith.

It is virtually impossible to know all of the factors behind a school problem, a needy parent, or a troublesome pupil. Therefore, to be personally invited by the Lord to come to Him, the Creator of life itself and to ask Him for wisdom to solve the problem is one of the greatest proofs of His love for us.

Bow now before our Heavenly Father; thank Him for His great, unsearchable love for you, and ask Him personally for a fresh supply of wisdom for this day. Then make this a constant prayer request daily, since He does want to give you this wisdom liberally.

Ye have not . . . because ye ask not!

44

COURAGE . . . DON'T ASK!

Be strong and of good courage, fear not, nor be afraid of them; for the Lord thy God he it is that doth go with thee; he will not fail thee, nor forsake thee.

And Moses called unto Joshua, and said unto him in the sight of all Israel. *Be strong and of good courage:* for thou must go with this people unto the land which the Lord hath sworn unto their fathers to give them: and thou shalt cause them to inherit it. *Deuteronomy 31:6, 7*

Nowhere in God's Word does it indicate that you should ask for courage! The numerous portions of Scripture that refer to courage always state . . . "take courage" . . . "be of good courage" . . . and so forth. Wisdom and understanding may be requested of God (James 1:5, I Kings 3:9) but not courage. Please do not ask . . . take it.

So often we pray, plan, and decide before God that a certain policy or procedure should be initiated; however, it does not materialize. Why? Perhaps we had no confidence to take the first step of faith. In prayer our eyes were fixed on God . . . later we looked within ourselves and our heart sank. Remember Peter when he looked upon Christ and walked on the sea; then he looked at the waves . . . and the sea walked on him.

The Apostle Paul said in Philippians 4:13, "I can do all things through Christ who strengthens me."

We need to step out in sheer courage and faith, and test our wonderful God. Remember, some of the things that do not require courage are: quitting when the going gets rough; meeting evil with evil; purchasing needed equipment when you know exactly where the money is coming from; buying land or building buildings *after* you get the entire cost pledged.

The cemetery is full of many graves of Christians who slipped through life making as few waves as possible. They died in obscurity when all the time God had other plans for them . . . they would not take the first step.

True courage is the result of scriptural fortitude based on God's Word. Apply sound reasoning to all your tasks. Purpose in your heart that you will pray, plan . . . and proceed, knowing that God will direct. Only you can take courage within yourself.

45

THE STUDENT BECOMES LIKE THE TEACHER

Only take heed to thyself, and keep thy soul diligently, lest thou forget the things which thine eyes have seen, and lest they depart from thy heart all the days of thy life: but teach them thy sons, and thy sons' sons;

Specially the day that thou stoodest before the Lord thy God in Horeb, when the Lord said unto me, gather me the people together, and I will make them hear my words, that they may learn to fear me all the days that they shall live upon the earth, and that they may teach their children.
Deuteronomy 4:9, 10

The day began in a very normal way but when it was concluded, I had to admit it had turned into quite an unusual one. It was the first time that I had interviewed a parent couple who agreed with the school's purposes for their child but not for themselves. Mr. and Mrs. Bartender wanted to enroll their little six-year old in our first grade. Both parents were active in their bar business and had no time for church or for spiritual things. However, they wanted to be sure their girl was not heading for the same future they were experiencing. Therefore, they wanted her to get our good academic training as well as the "religious" instruction.

As the discussion progressed, I assured them that what they were seeking was impossible. Their girl was "doomed" to be exactly like them! I mentioned that the student becomes like the teacher. In the training program, the leader is the example by word and by deed. The pupil cannot help but become like his instructor. This is why the home is so essential in the patterning of our children. I said to this couple that the only way to change or shape their girl to the kind of person they wanted was to be that kind of person themselves.

I explained that the "new life" begins as one receives Jesus Christ as Saviour. Then as one yields his whole life to the Holy Spirit, the Holy Spirit starts to change and reshape that one to be like Jesus. This change of life will have the greatest positive impact upon a child. The parents did not accept God's truths because they would have had to give up "too much." They left by saying to me that I did not want to help their child. I said we certainly did want to help, but they did not want to pay the price for a "Christ-centered home." However, the real tragedy of the story is that *they will pay the price*, a dear one, for not having Christ as the Head of their lives.

The challenge to us, as Christian teachers, is that while we are the child's school parents each day, our lives must be of the highest caliber. Our pupils are becoming like us.

Do you want your students to be exactly like you? If not, then the change in your life must be made under the scrutiny and conviction of the Holy Spirit. You must begin with I John 1:9 and continue from there, in honesty and diligence to seek Him and His wisdom for change.

46

TEACHING TRUTHS TRUTHFULLY

For not the hearers of the law are just before God, the doers of the law shall be justified.

And art confident that thou thyself are a guide of the blind, a light of them which are in darkness.

An instructor of the foolish, a teacher of babes, which has the form of knowledge and of the truth in the law.

Thou therefore which teachest another, teachest thou not thyself? thou that preachest a man should not steal, dost thou steal?

Thou that sayest a man should not commit adultery, dost thou commit adultery? thou that abhorrest idols, dost thou commit sacrilege?

Thou that makest thy boast of the law, through breaking the law dishonourest thou God? *Romans 2:13, 19-23*

We are reminded in many portions of God's Word that we are to be doers of the Word and not hearers only! However, we may not realize that it is impossible to be an effective teacher of the Word without being a doer! There is a certain deep-seated communication skill one has when sharing or explaining a truth that has been experienced. The same truth can be revealed by a much more competent teacher with years of classroom maturity without making the slightest impression.

The children in our classes may or may not be able to tell whether we have experienced the truth we are teaching, but the real test is the impact the truth makes on them. Every teacher wants the Word of God to really take hold in the children's lives. In fact, one of the chief concerns upon the heart of many teachers is that they do not see their students being greatly affected by the Word. Bible lessons are prepared carefully and skillfully, but may make no impact upon the heart. Facts can reach the mind to be stored for the future, but truth that reaches the heart will result in action immediately.

When we are talking about joy and happiness in Christ, are we really happy in Christ? When we explain faith, are we harboring fear and doubt in our hearts about a home problem? When we discuss forgiveness, are there those within or without the school whom we have not forgiven? When we challenge our children to witness and win others to Christ, are we winning others? When we stress how important prayer and Bible reading are, do we devote the time in each area as we should? The list of additional truths that we teach daily could go on and on. However, the important question is, have we experienced or are we experiencing the truth we are presenting? If we have not, then our teaching is carrying very little weight in the lives of the children. A trick of Satan is to have us skip over those truths not experienced, while the Lord desires that we try Him and yield to Him, so He can work through us in every area.

God wants to teach every truth To You and Through You.

"For not the hearers of the law (or the teachers) are just before God, but the DOERS of the law shall be justified."

47

GOD'S SERVANT MUST NOT STRIVE

And the servant of the Lord must not strive; but be gentle unto all men, apt to teach, patient,

In meekness instructing those that oppose themselves; if God peradventure will give them repentance to the acknowledging of the truth;

And that they may recover themselves out of the snare of the devil, who are taken captive by him at his will.

II Timothy 2:24-26

As servants of the Lord, we are commanded not to strive. We must not find ourselves in physical or mental wrestling matches with our peers, parents, or pupils. It is amazing when one realizes the magnitude of inter-personal relationships that could take place each day within the confines of the school scene. To get an idea of the potential number, follow this formula: take the number of teachers and multiply that number by the number of students; then multiply your answer by the parents in the school; then finish by multiplying your answer by the nonteaching staff and your school board members. The result is that number of potential friction points that can develop. It is very easy to suddenly find yourself in mental combat with one or more individuals over one or more issues. *The servant of the Lord must not strive!*

Proverbs 16:7 states, "When a man's ways please the Lord, he maketh even his enemies to be at peace with him."

We must by all means walk a path each day

that pleases the Lord, and then let the circumstances fall in place without our worry. God tells us this in many ways:

Envy is the rottenness of the bones (Prov. 14:30).

He that is soon angry dealeth foolishly (Prov. 14:17).

A soft answer turneth away wrath (Prov. 15:1).

A man that hath friends must shew himself friendly (Prov. 18:24).

Beloved, let us love one another (I John 4:7).

Let us therefore follow after the things which make for peace (Rom. 14:19).

These are only a portion of many scriptural principles that, if followed, will reduce greatly the tension that normally builds during the day. We must conscientiously employ each truth we know; otherwise, we invite strife.

When we speak of resting in the Lord and having confidence in God, we are ultimately speaking of His Word. It is this Word that reinforces our assurance and gives the peace of heart we need to quench strife. So rather than fume or fuss, mentally or verbally, we should yield to the Holy Spirit and let key truths fill our thoughts.

Trouble and anguish have taken hold on me: yet thy commandments are my delights (Ps. 119:143).

The entrance of thy words giveth light: it giveth understanding unto the simple (Ps. 119:130).

Each day your work is to be exciting and fruitful. Problems and challenges are to be expected and welcomed, and through patience, prayer, planning, hard work, and God's principles, you can be effective without striving.

48

RISE AND SHINE

Arise, shine; for thy light is come, and the glory of the Lord is risen upon thee.

For, behold, the darkness shall cover the earth, and gross darkness the people: but the Lord shall arise upon thee, and his glory shall be seen upon thee.

And the Gentiles shall come to thy light, and kings to the brightness of thy rising. *Isaiah 60:1-3*

Many of the very familiar sayings of the day originated in God's Word. "Rise and shine" indeed has a good scriptural base. As educators for Christ, we need so definitely to *go* and to *glow* with the gospel. Jesus said, "that they may see your good works, and glorify your Father which is in heaven."

As one can see from this verse, it is the light of one's countenance that illuminates his good works. In other words, our good works for God will be displayed if we let our light shine. Where does one get the light? From the Son . . . of course!

As a Christian spends time with the Lord and lets His Word richly dwell in him and through him, he begins to shine with His love.

As we begin our classes each day, there must be a "glow" in our faces. The children are so perceptive to see it as it appears or as it . . . disappears. Children have a "spiritual radar" system that outdoes any adult sensitivity. If we are teaching facts daily with no "go" (enthusiasm) or no "glow" (love), then do not expect the students to reflect *anything*. Remember . . . our good works of faithful lesson planning, and so forth, must all be lighted by us! "Let your light so shine, that they may see your good works."

The day will be filled with many, many duties. Some of the work is pleasant and happy, and other duties are hard and cumbersome. All will be done in some sort of attitude. I Corinthians 16:14 says, "Let all your things be done with charity." The Lord knows that if anything is going to be effective for His glory, it has to be done in love.

The Lord is my light (Ps. 27:1), and entrance of thy Word giveth light.

It is, therefore, imperative that you spend enough time with the Lord each day in prayer and with His Word, allowing the Son to shine through you to your students which will produce good fruit in them for His glory.

49

ONE STORY ONLY

In the mean time, when there were gathered together an innumerable multitude of people, insomuch that they trode one upon another, he began to say unto his disciples first of all, Beware ye of the leaven of the Pharisees, which is hypocrisy.

For there is nothing covered, that shall not be revealed; neither hid, that shall not be known.

Therefore whatsoever ye have spoken in darkness shall be heard in the light; and that which ye have spoken in the ear in closets shall be proclaimed upon the housetops.

Luke 12:1-3

One day as I sat at the "Administrative Council" table (this was the entire group of school administrators within the public school system of a certain district), the superintendent made a startling statement. At the time we were discussing a problem within the district. He told our group that he had a certain story for the school board and another story for the parents of the schools. He was openly admitting he was a hypocrite!

Jesus warns us sharply to beware of this awful "leaven" of the Pharisees. To engage in this deadly game of different stories to different people in our daily school work weakens greatly our very faith. It appears we can trust the Lord for the most crucial thing in all the world, His eternal life, His salvation; but cannot trust Him to work out a simple, but sticky school problem. To face a parent, teacher, principal, or board member with the truth can often be extremely difficult. It is so much easier to change the story around or leave out certain points to gain a favorable image, but is it worth the loss of integrity? Sooner or later the picture becomes clear and great damage has been done.

On the other hand, I do feel that a loving Christian will always strive to be tactful and careful in all situations. I am not advocating a harsh "care-about-no-one-attitude." This certainly would not be the love of Christ in action. Jesus was always truthful with great compassion. He knew He was in His Father's will, so He spoke firmly with great clarity to the Pharisees; to the woman at the well; to the rich young ruler; to Nicodemus; and to the lawyer. In each case the truth as a "bitter pill" to the recipient, but it eventually brought joy to those that received it.

In school situations occurring daily when problems arise, there really is only one story or explanation, the true one as it honestly happened. If you do not see the whole story, then do not fill in with your personal feelings. Allow the story to remain partial, admitting it to be so.

As a Christian, your only true foundation in Jesus Christ is based on truth and integrity. Psalm 11:3 states it so profoundly, "If the foundations be destroyed, what can the righteous do?"

In your work today as a Christian teacher, rejoice that you have begun your spiritual life with the truth, even Jesus Christ. Maintain the truth in all endeavors and see the Lord do miracles daily as He accomplishes His purpose.

50

WHAT HAS HE DONE FOR YOU!

And Jesus went out, and his disciples, into the towns of Caesarea Philippi: and by the way he asked his disciples, saying unto them, Whom do men say that I am?

And they answered, John the Baptist: but some say Elias; and others, One of the prophets.

And he saith unto them, But whom say ye that I am? And Peter answereth and saith unto him, Thou art the Christ.

Mark 8:27-29

What has the Lord done for you? We may quickly respond, "Why, He's blessed us with a good staff, a nice building, plenty of students, cooperative parents," and so forth.

These certainly are some excellent blessings from the Lord, but the question has not been answered. What has He done for *you?* If you can begin to enumerate the various ways God has *recently* blessed and provided for you, you are a prime witness! You need to be on the front line of sharing with others. You will encourage and inspire other staff to a higher level of thinking and working with your good word. Children are always eager to hear of *actual* events and *live* incidents of the ways God is moving. One of the fastest and most effective ways to "turn on" people is to relate a specific blessing that the Lord has bestowed. We need to be a fountain that is taking in fresh water and spouting it forth to quench the thirst of barren and needy souls. Keep your heart open to receive the blessings of God, to share and pass on to others, that they may respond. "The Lord hath done great things for them" (Ps. 126:2).

If your answer to the question, "What has the Lord done for you?" is rather negative, your daily ministry must needs be ineffective. No one can have the joy of Christ and a good outflow of the abundant life without experiencing God's continuous hand of blessing. If we are not receptive to the Holy Spirit's leading daily, we cannot give freely. We can give only what we have!

The "inner glow" and the "outer go" are all linked with God's Word. As you read prayerfully and heed carefully ... being doers of the Word, God's miracles become evident. You will see His Hand daily, even hourly, on your life. Your fleshly eyes will become spiritually sharp. Then you will be able to share the precious promises and the wondrous blessings of God. What has He done for you ... personally? Why not test the Lord so you can see Him work. ...

CONCLUSION

Working in a Christian school is a very exciting experience. It captures all the elements that make any job worthwhile and productive. I trust that in preceding pages you have caught glimpses of these scriptural essentials as God has revealed them to you. Go over the devotional thoughts again and again, allowing the Holy Spirit to indelibly imprint His Word and His principles on your "teaching" heart.

You, as a Christian teacher, have a high calling from God. You must have recognized God's love and confidence in you to enable you to do this vital work. Accordingly, nothing should stand in your way in praying and seeking God's guidance . . . for being positive, for rejoicing, and for training boys and girls in the way they should go . . . God's way!

Let's "pre-prayer" together . . . as you . . .

Teach Them Diligently

—Art Nazigian